100 BEST
4 Ingredient Recipes

pil

Publications
International, Ltd.

Favorite Brand Name Recipes at www.fbnr.com

Pictured on the front cover: Grilled Sherry Pork Chop *(page 108).*
Pictured on the back cover *(top to bottom):* Velveeta® Ultimate Macaroni & Cheese *(page 44)* and Bacon-Wrapped Breadsticks *(page 6).*

ISBN-13: 978-0-7853-8051-1
ISBN-10: 0-7853-8051-5

Library of Congress Control Number: 2002110213

Manufactured in China.

8 7 6 5 4 3 2 1

Microwave Cooking: Microwave ovens vary in wattage. Use the cooking times as guidelines and check for doneness before adding more time.

Preparation/Cooking Times: Preparation times are based on the approximate amount of time required to assemble the recipe before cooking, baking, chilling or serving. These times include preparation steps such as measuring, chopping and mixing. The fact that some preparations and cooking can be done simultaneously is taken into account. Preparation of optional ingredients and serving suggestions is not included.

Contents

Introduction   4

Alluring Appetizers   6

Satisfying Side Dishes   28

Tempting Poultry   54

Enticing Beef   84

Phenomenal Pork   108

Pleasing Fish & Shellfish   128

Playful Kid Food   148

Dashing Desserts   184

Acknowledgments   218

Index   219

Metric Chart   224

Introduction

Make meal planning easier with less ingredients! Cooking and baking can be difficult if there are too many ingredients to shop for, measure and prepare. Working with just four ingredients takes the stress out of cooking and the meal is ready in less time.

The following pages are filled with the simplest easy-to-prepare recipes around. Most of these recipes include only four ingredients. That's right! Just four ingredients are needed to prepare delicious meals. There are, however, some recipes that have a few more than 4 ingredients. We aren't counting salt, pepper, water, nonstick cooking spray and small amounts of oil, ingredients you have on hand. Remember also, that ingredients marked as "optional" or "for garnish" aren't included in the four ingredient count—add them to make your meal extra special. These "extra" ingredients will add little time into your preparation since the amounts are so small.

This book is designed not only to make the recipes effortless, but to make finding the perfect one to use easy as well. The book is divided into eight organized chapters, from appetizers for get-togethers to chicken or pork dishes for the family. Another way to make cooking extra simple is by using the index. For example, if you have a certain ingredient on hand and want to use it for your meal, simply find the ingredient in the index and you will find many recipes to choose from. How much easier can cooking be?

Become the star of the kitchen when you serve these delicious dishes. No one will ever believe they were prepared with just FOUR ingredients!

Alluring
APPETIZERS

Bacon-Wrapped Breadsticks

8 slices bacon
16 garlic-flavored breadsticks (about 8 inches long)
¾ cup grated Parmesan cheese
2 tablespoons chopped fresh parsley (optional)

Cut bacon slices in half lengthwise. Wrap half slice of bacon diagonally around each breadstick. Combine Parmesan cheese and parsley, if desired, in shallow dish; set aside.

Place 4 breadsticks on double layer of paper towels in microwave oven. Microwave on HIGH 2 to 3 minutes or until bacon is cooked through. Immediately roll breadsticks in Parmesan mixture to coat. Repeat with remaining breadsticks. *Makes 16 breadsticks*

Bacon-Wrapped Breadsticks

Sunshine Chicken Drumsticks

½ cup A.1.® Steak Sauce
¼ cup ketchup
¼ cup apricot preserves
12 chicken drumsticks (about 2½ pounds)

Blend steak sauce, ketchup and preserves in small bowl with wire whisk until smooth. Brush chicken with sauce.

Grill chicken over medium heat for 20 minutes or until no longer pink, turning and brushing with remaining sauce. (Do not baste during last 5 minutes of grilling.) Serve hot. *Makes 12 appetizers*

Buffalo-Style Shrimp

⅓ cup *Frank's® RedHot® Cayenne Pepper Sauce*
⅓ cup butter or margarine, melted
1 pound raw large shrimp, shelled and deveined
2 ribs celery, cut into large pieces

1. Combine *Frank's RedHot* Sauce and butter in small bowl. Alternately thread shrimp and celery onto metal skewers. Place in shallow bowl. Pour ⅓ cup *Frank's RedHot* Sauce mixture over kabobs. Cover; refrigerate 30 minutes. Prepare grill.

2. Grill,* over medium coals, 3 to 5 minutes or until shrimp are opaque. Heat remaining *Frank's RedHot* Sauce mixture; pour over shrimp and celery. *Makes 4 servings*

Or, broil 6-inches from heat.

Prep Time: 10 minutes
Marinate Time: 30 minutes
Cook Time: 5 minutes

Sunshine Chicken Drumsticks

Arizona Cheese Crisp

Vegetable oil for deep-frying
2 (10- or 12-inch) flour tortillas
1 to 1½ cups (4 to 6 ounces) shredded Cheddar or
    Monterey Jack cheese
½ cup picante sauce
¼ cup grated Parmesan cheese

Pour oil into wok to depth of 1 inch. Place over medium-high heat until oil registers 360°F on deep-frying thermometer. Slide 1 tortilla into oil. Using 2 slotted spoons, gently hold center of tortilla down so oil flows over edges. When tortilla is crisp and golden on bottom, carefully tilt wok, holding tortilla in place with spoon, to cover edge of tortilla with oil; cook until lightly browned. Rotate tortilla as needed so entire edge is lightly browned. Remove from oil and drain on paper towels, curled side down. Repeat with second tortilla. Tortillas can be made up to 8 hours in advance. Cover loosely and let stand at room temperature.

Preheat oven to 350°F. Place shells, curled side up, on baking sheet. Sprinkle each with half of the Cheddar cheese; top each with half of the picante sauce. Sprinkle with Parmesan cheese. Bake, uncovered, 8 to 10 minutes or until cheeses melt. To serve, break into bite-size pieces. *Makes 4 to 6 servings*

Chorizo Cheese Crisp: Remove casing from ¼ pound chorizo sausage. Crumble sausage into large skillet; stir over medium-high heat until browned. Drain fat. Follow directions for Arizona Cheese Crisp but substitute chorizo for Parmesan cheese.

Olive Cheese Crisp: Follow directions for Arizona Cheese Crisp but omit picante sauce and Parmesan cheese. Sprinkle ⅓ cup sliced pitted ripe olives and ⅓ cup diced green chilies over Cheddar cheese.

Arizona Cheese Crisp

Can't Get Enough Chicken Wings

18 chicken wings (about 3 pounds)
 1 envelope LIPTON® RECIPE SECRETS® Savory Herb with Garlic
   Soup Mix
 ½ cup water
 2 to 3 tablespoons hot pepper sauce* (optional)
 2 tablespoons margarine or butter

*Use more or less hot pepper sauce as desired.

1. Cut tips off chicken wings (save tips for soup). Cut chicken wings in half at joint. Deep fry, bake or broil until golden brown and crunchy.

2. Meanwhile, in small saucepan, combine soup mix, water and hot pepper sauce. Cook over low heat, stirring occasionally, 2 minutes or until thickened. Remove from heat and stir in margarine.

3. In large bowl, toss cooked chicken wings with hot soup mixture until evenly coated. Serve, if desired, over greens with cut-up celery.

Makes 36 appetizers

quick tip

The tips from the chicken wings can be used to make your own chicken stock. Simmer wing tips with water, onion, celery, bay leaf and any other vegetables or herbs you desire for 1 to 2 hours. Strain stock and skim off the fat. Freeze in containers or self-closing plastic bags for later use.

Zesty Bruschetta

**1 envelope LIPTON® RECIPE SECRETS® Savory Herb with Garlic
   Soup Mix**
6 tablespoons olive or vegetable oil*
**1 loaf French or Italian bread (about 18 inches long), sliced
   lengthwise**
2 tablespoons shredded or grated Parmesan cheese

*Substitution: Use ½ cup margarine or butter, melted.

Preheat oven to 350°F. Blend savory herb with garlic soup mix and oil.
Brush onto bread, then sprinkle with cheese.

Bake 12 minutes or until golden. Slice, then serve.

Makes 1 loaf, about 18 pieces

Broccoli-Cheese Quesadillas

1 cup (4 ounces) shredded nonfat Cheddar cheese
½ cup finely chopped fresh broccoli
2 tablespoons picante sauce or salsa
4 (6- to 7-inch) corn or flour tortillas
1 teaspoon margarine, divided

1. Combine cheese, broccoli and picante sauce in small bowl;
mix well.

2. Spoon ¼ of the cheese mixture onto 1 side of each tortilla; fold
tortilla over filling.

3. Melt ½ teaspoon margarine in 10-inch nonstick skillet over medium
heat. Add 2 quesadillas; cook about 2 minutes on each side or until
tortillas are golden brown and cheese is melted. Repeat with
remaining margarine and quesadillas. Cool completely.

Makes 4 servings

Tip: Refrigerate individually wrapped quesadillas up to 2 days or
freeze up to 3 weeks.

Mexican Roll-Ups

6 uncooked lasagna noodles
¾ cup prepared guacamole
¾ cup chunky salsa
¾ cup (3 ounces) shredded nonfat Cheddar cheese
  Additional salsa (optional)

1. Cook lasagna noodles according to package directions, omitting salt. Rinse with cool water; drain. Cool.

2. Spread 2 tablespoons guacamole onto each noodle; top each with 2 tablespoons salsa and 2 tablespoons cheese.

3. Roll up noodles jelly-roll fashion. Cut each roll-up in half to form two equal-size roll-ups. Serve immediately with salsa or cover with plastic wrap and refrigerate up to 3 hours.   *Makes 12 appetizers*

quick tip

> To prepare your own guacamole, combine 2 mashed large avocados, ¼ cup finely chopped tomato, 2 tablespoons grated onion, 2 tablespoons lime juice, ½ teaspoon salt and ¼ teaspoon hot pepper sauce. Add black pepper to taste; mix well.

Mexican Roll-Ups

Cheddar Tomato Bacon Toasts

1 jar (16 ounces) RAGÚ® Cheese Creations!® Double Cheddar Sauce
1 medium tomato, chopped
5 slices bacon, crisp-cooked and crumbled (about ⅓ cup)
2 loaves Italian bread (each about 16 inches long), each cut into
**   16 slices**

1. Preheat oven to 350°F. In medium bowl, combine Ragú® Cheese Creations! Sauce, tomato and bacon.

2. On baking sheet, arrange bread slices. Evenly top with sauce mixture.

3. Bake 10 minutes or until sauce mixture is bubbling. Serve immediately.   *Makes 16 servings*

Prep Time: 10 minutes
Cook Time: 10 minutes

Cheddar Tomato Bacon Toasts

Hidden Valley Ranch® Cheese Fingers

2 small loaves French bread (8 ounces each), cut in half lengthwise
1 package (8 ounces) cream cheese or Neufchâtel cheese
1 packet (1 ounce) HIDDEN VALLEY® The Original Ranch® Salad
    Dressing & Seasoning Mix
4 cups assorted toppings, such as chopped onions, chopped bell
    peppers and grated cheese

Slice bread crosswise into 1-inch fingers, leaving fingers attached. Mix cream cheese and salad dressing & seasoning mix together. Spread on cut sides of bread. Pile on toppings. Broil until brown and bubbly.

Makes about 4½ dozen fingers

Chili Garlic Prawns

2 tablespoons vegetable oil
1 pound prawns, peeled and deveined
3 tablespoons LEE KUM KEE® Chili Garlic Sauce
1 green onion, cut into slices

1. Heat oil in wok or skillet.

2. Add prawns and stir-fry until just pink.

3. Add chili garlic sauce and stir-fry until prawns are completely cooked.

4. Sprinkle with green onion and serve.   *Makes 4 servings*

Roasted Sweet Pepper Tapas

2 red bell peppers (8 ounces each)
1 clove garlic, minced
1 teaspoon chopped fresh oregano leaves *or* ½ teaspoon dried
oregano leaves, crushed
2 tablespoons olive oil
  Garlic bread (optional)
  Fresh oregano sprig for garnish

1. Cover broiler pan with foil. Adjust rack so that broiler pan is about 4 inches from heat source. Preheat broiler. Place peppers on foil. Broil 15 to 20 minutes until blackened on all sides, turning peppers every 5 minutes with tongs.

2. To steam peppers and loosen skin, place blackened peppers in paper bag. Close bag; set aside to cool about 15 to 20 minutes.

3. To peel peppers, cut around core, twist and remove. Cut peppers in half; place pepper halves on cutting board. Peel off skin with paring knife; rinse under cold water to remove seeds.

4. Lay halves flat and slice lengthwise into ¼-inch strips.

5. Transfer pepper strips to glass jar. Add garlic, oregano and oil. Close lid; shake to blend. Marinate at least 1 hour. Serve on plates with garlic bread or refrigerate in jar up to 1 week. Garnish, if desired.
Makes 6 appetizer servings

quick tip

Use this roasting technique for all types of sweet and hot peppers. Broiling time will vary depending on size of pepper. When handling hot peppers, such as Anaheim, jalapeño, poblano or serrano, wear plastic disposable gloves and use caution to prevent irritation of skin or eyes. Green bell peppers do not work as well since their skins are thinner.

Spinach Cheese Bundles

1 container (6½ ounces) garlic- and herb-flavored spreadable cheese
½ cup chopped fresh spinach
¼ teaspoon pepper
1 package (17¼ ounces) frozen puff pastry, thawed
  Sweet and sour or favorite dipping sauce (optional)

Preheat oven to 400°F. Combine spreadable cheese, spinach and pepper in small bowl; mix well.

Roll out one sheet puff pastry dough on floured surface into 12-inch square. Cut into 16 (3-inch) squares. Place about 1 teaspoon cheese mixture in center of each square. Brush edges of squares with water. Bring edges together up over filling and twist tightly to seal; fan out corners of puff pastry.

Place bundles 2 inches apart on baking sheet. Bake about 13 minutes or until golden brown. Repeat with remaining sheet of puff pastry and cheese mixture. Serve warm with dipping sauce, if desired.

Makes 32 bundles

Spinach Cheese Bundles

Baked Apricot Brie

1 round (8 ounce) Brie cheese
⅓ cup apricot preserves
2 tablespoons sliced almonds
   Cracked pepper or other assorted crackers

1. Preheat oven to 400°F. Place cheese in small baking pan; spread top of cheese with preserves and sprinkle with almonds.

2. Bake about 10 to 12 minutes or until cheese begins to melt and lose its shape. Serve hot with crackers. Refrigerate leftovers; reheat before serving.   *Makes 6 servings*

Cook Time: 12 minutes

quick tip

Brie is a soft-ripened, unpressed cheese made from cow's milk. It has a distinctive round shape, edible white rind and creamy yellow interior. Avoid Brie that has a chalky center (it is underripe) or a strong ammonia odor (it is overripe). The cheese should give slightly to pressure and have an evenly colored, barely moist rind.

Baked Apricot Brie

Hot & Spicy Buffalo Chicken Wings

1 can (15 ounces) DEL MONTE® Original Sloppy Joe Sauce
¼ cup thick and chunky salsa, medium
1 tablespoon red wine vinegar or cider vinegar
20 chicken wings (about 4 pounds)

1. Preheat oven to 400°F.

2. Combine sloppy joe sauce, salsa and vinegar in small bowl. Remove ¼ cup sauce mixture to serve with cooked chicken wings; cover and refrigerate. Set aside remaining sauce mixture.

3. Arrange wings in single layer in large, shallow baking pan; brush wings with remaining sauce mixture.

4. Bake chicken, uncovered, on middle rack in oven 35 minutes or until chicken is no longer pink in center, turning and brushing with remaining sauce mixture after 15 minutes. Serve with reserved ¼ cup sauce. Garnish, if desired. *Makes 4 servings*

Prep Time: 5 minutes
Cook Time: 35 minutes

Crostini

¼ loaf whole wheat baguette (4 ounces)
4 plum tomatoes
1 cup (4 ounces) shredded part-skim mozzarella cheese
3 tablespoons prepared pesto sauce

1. Preheat oven to 400°F. Slice baguette into 16 very thin, diagonal slices. Slice each tomato vertically into four ¼-inch slices.

2. Place baguette slices on nonstick baking sheet. Top each with 1 tablespoon cheese, then 1 slice tomato. Bake about 8 minutes or until bread is lightly toasted and cheese is melted. Remove from oven; top each crostini with about ½ teaspoon pesto sauce. Garnish with fresh basil, if desired. Serve warm. *Makes 8 appetizer servings*

BelGioioso® Fontina Melt

1 loaf Italian or French bread
2 fresh tomatoes, cubed
Basil leaves, julienned
BELGIOIOSO® Fontina Cheese, sliced

Cut bread lengthwise into halves. Top each half with tomatoes and sprinkle with basil. Top with BelGioioso Fontina Cheese. Place in oven at 350°F for 10 to 12 minutes or until cheese is golden brown.
Makes 6 to 8 servings

Super Nachos

12 large baked low-fat tortilla chips (about 1½ ounces)
½ cup (2 ounces) shredded reduced-fat Cheddar cheese
¼ cup fat-free refried beans
2 tablespoons chunky salsa

1. Arrange chips in single layer on large microwavable plate. Sprinkle cheese evenly over chips.

2. Spoon teaspoonfuls of beans over chips; top with ½ teaspoonfuls of salsa.

3. Microwave at MEDIUM (50%) 1½ minutes; rotate dish. Microwave 1 to 1½ minutes or until cheese is melted.   *Makes 2 servings*

Conventional Oven Directions: Substitute foil-covered baking sheet for microwavable plate. Assemble nachos as directed on prepared baking sheet. Bake at 350°F for 10 to 12 minutes or until cheese is melted.

quick tip

> For a single serving of nachos, arrange 6 large tortilla chips on microwavable plate; top with ¼ cup cheese, 2 tablespoons refried beans and 1 tablespoon salsa. Microwave at MEDIUM (50%) 1 minute; rotate dish. Continue to microwave 30 seconds to 1 minute or until cheese is melted.

Super Nachos

Satisfying
SIDE DISHES

Fast Pesto Focaccia

1 can (10 ounces) pizza crust dough
2 tablespoons prepared pesto
4 sun-dried tomatoes packed in oil, drained

1. Preheat oven to 425°F. Lightly grease 8×8×2-inch pan. Unroll pizza dough; fold in half and pat into pan.

2. Spread pesto evenly over dough. Chop tomatoes or snip with kitchen scissors; sprinkle over pesto. Press tomatoes into dough. Make indentations in dough every 2 inches using wooden spoon handle.

3. Bake 10 to 12 minutes or until golden brown. Cut into squares and serve warm or at room temperature.

Makes 16 squares

Prep and Cook Time: 20 minutes

Fast Pesto Focaccia

Herbed Corn on the Cob

1 tablespoon butter or margarine
1 teaspoon mixed dried herb leaves, such as basil, oregano, sage
    and rosemary
⅛ teaspoon salt
  Black pepper
4 ears corn, husks removed

MICROWAVE DIRECTIONS

1. Combine butter, herbs, salt and pepper in small microwavable bowl. Microwave at MEDIUM (50%) 30 to 45 seconds or until butter is melted.

2. With pastry brush, coat corn with butter mixture. Place corn on microwavable plate; microwave at HIGH 5 to 6 minutes. Turn corn over and microwave at HIGH 5 to 6 minutes until tender.

Makes 4 servings

Onion-Roasted Potatoes

1 envelope LIPTON® RECIPE SECRETS® Onion Soup Mix*
4 medium all-purpose potatoes, cut into large chunks (about
    2 pounds)
⅓ cup olive or vegetable oil

Also terrific with LIPTON® RECIPE SECRETS® Onion Mushroom, Golden Onion or Savory Herb with Garlic Soup Mix.

1. Preheat oven to 450°F. In large plastic bag or bowl, add all ingredients. Close bag and shake, or toss in bowl, until potatoes are evenly coated.

2. In 13×9-inch baking or roasting pan, arrange potatoes; discard bag.

3. Bake uncovered, stirring occasionally, 40 minutes or until potatoes are tender and golden brown.
Makes 4 servings

Herbed Corn on the Cob

Satisfying Side Dishes

Cottage Fried Potatoes

Canola oil
3 to 4 russet potatoes (about 1½ pounds), cut into wedges
Coarse salt

1. Preheat oven to warm. Line 2 large baking sheets with paper towels; set aside.

2. Pour oil into large deep skillet or wok to 1-inch depth. Attach deep-fry or candy thermometer to side of skillet, making sure bulb is submerged in oil but not touching bottom of skillet. Heat oil over high heat until thermometer registers 390°F.

3. Carefully slide 8 to 10 potato wedges into skillet. (Do not crowd skillet or oil will lose too much heat.) Reduce heat to medium-high; cook about 4 minutes or until potatoes are deep golden brown and skins are crispy, turning gently to separate wedges so that they cook evenly.

4. Carefully remove potatoes and arrange in single layer on baking sheet. Blot excess oil from potatoes. Place baking sheet in oven to keep potatoes warm.

5. Repeat steps 2 through 4 with remaining potatoes. Sprinkle potatoes with salt to taste. Serve hot. *Makes 4 to 6 servings*

French Onion Bread Stix

1⅓ cups *French's®* **French Fried Onions, crushed**
¼ cup grated Parmesan cheese
1 container (11 ounces) refrigerated soft bread sticks
1 egg white, beaten

1. Preheat oven to 350°F. Combine French Fried Onions and cheese in pie plate. Separate dough into 12 pieces on sheet of waxed paper.

2. Brush one side of dough with egg white. Dip pieces, wet sides down, into crumbs, pressing firmly. Baste top surface with egg white and dip into crumbs.

3. Twist pieces to form spirals. Arrange on ungreased baking sheet. Bake 15 to 20 minutes or until golden brown.

Makes 12 bread sticks

Prep Time: 5 minutes
Cook Time: 15 minutes

1-2-3 Cheddar Broccoli Casserole

1 jar (16 ounces) RAGÚ® Cheese Creations!® Double Cheddar Sauce
2 boxes (10 ounces each) frozen broccoli florets, thawed
¼ cup plain or Italian seasoned dry bread crumbs
1 tablespoon margarine or butter, melted

1. Preheat oven to 350°F. In 1½-quart casserole, combine Ragú Cheese Creations! Sauce and broccoli.

2. Evenly top with bread crumbs combined with margarine.

3. Bake uncovered 20 minutes or until bread crumbs are golden and broccoli is tender.   *Makes 6 servings*

Prep Time: 5 minutes
Cook Time: 20 minutes

quick tip

> Substitute your favorite frozen vegetables or vegetable blend for broccoli florets.

1-2-3 Cheddar Broccoli Casserole

Brown Rice Royal

2 cups (about 8 ounces) sliced fresh mushrooms
½ cup thinly sliced green onions
1 tablespoon vegetable oil
3 cups cooked brown rice (cooked in beef broth)

Cook mushrooms and onions in oil in large skillet over medium-high heat until tender. Add rice. Stir until thoroughly heated.

Makes 6 servings

Microwave Directions: Combine mushrooms, onions and oil in 2-quart microproof baking dish. Cook on HIGH (100% power) 2 to 3 minutes. Add rice; continue to cook on HIGH 3 to 4 minutes, stirring after 2 minutes, or until thoroughly heated.

*Favorite recipe from **USA Rice Federation***

Creamed Spinach Casserole

2 packages (10 ounces each) frozen chopped spinach, thawed, well drained
2 packages (8 ounces each) PHILADELPHIA® Cream Cheese, softened
1 teaspoon lemon and pepper seasoning salt
⅓ cup crushed seasoned croutons

MIX spinach, cream cheese and seasoning salt until well blended.

SPOON into 1-quart casserole. Sprinkle with crushed croutons.

BAKE at 350°F for 25 to 30 minutes or until thoroughly heated.

Makes 6 to 8 servings

Prep Time: 10 minutes
Bake Time: 30 minutes

Brown Rice Royal

Classic Polenta

6 cups water
2 teaspoons salt
2 cups yellow cornmeal
¼ cup vegetable oil

1. Bring water and salt to a boil in large, heavy saucepan over medium-high heat. Stirring water vigorously, add cornmeal in very thin but steady stream (do not let lumps form). Reduce heat to low.

2. Cook polenta, uncovered, 40 to 60 minutes until very thick, stirring frequently. Polenta is ready when spoon will stand upright by itself in center of mixture. Polenta can be served at this point.*

3. For fried polenta, spray 11×7-inch baking pan with nonstick cooking spray. Spread polenta mixture evenly into baking pan. Cover and let stand at room temperature at least 6 hours or until completely cooled and firm.

4. Unmold polenta onto cutting board. Cut polenta crosswise into 1¼-inch-wide strips. Cut strips into 2- to 3-inch-long pieces.

5. Heat oil in large, heavy skillet over medium-high heat; reduce heat to medium. Fry polenta pieces, ½ at a time, 4 to 5 minutes until golden on all sides, turning as needed. Garnish as desired.

Makes 6 to 8 servings

*Polenta is an important component of Northern Italian cooking. The basic preparation presented here can be served in two forms. Hot freshly made polenta, prepared through step 2, can be mixed with ⅓ cup butter and ⅓ cup grated Parmesan cheese and served as a first course. Or, pour onto a large platter and top with a hearty meat sauce for a main dish. Fried polenta, as prepared here, is appropriate as an appetizer or as a side dish with meat.

Classic Polenta

Herbed Green Beans

1 pound fresh green beans, stem ends removed
1 teaspoon extra virgin olive oil
2 tablespoons chopped fresh basil *or* 2 teaspoons dried basil leaves

1. Steam green beans 5 minutes or until crisp-tender. Rinse under cold running water; drain and set aside.

2. Just before serving, heat oil over medium-low heat in large nonstick skillet. Add basil; cook and stir 1 minute, then add green beans. Cook until heated through. Garnish with additional fresh basil, if desired. Serve immediately.   *Makes 6 servings*

quick tip

When buying green beans, look for vivid green, crisp beans without scars. Pods should be well shaped and slim with small seeds. Buy beans of uniform size to ensure even cooking, and avoid bruised or large beans.

Garlic Bread

6 whole heads of garlic
1 teaspoon dried oregano leaves
4½ teaspoons extra virgin olive oil
1 loaf, unsliced, crusty sourdough or French bread, cut horizontally in half (1½ pounds)
Black pepper

1. Preheat oven to 350°F. Cut tops off heads of garlic and peel each head. Place heads, cut sides up, in small baking pan and sprinkle with oregano. Cover tightly with foil and bake 30 minutes. Uncover and bake 30 minutes more. Remove from oven, cool until easy to handle.

2. Carefully squeeze soft roasted garlic out of each clove to yield about ¾ cup. Place in blender or food processor; add oil and process until smooth.

3. Spread garlic mixture evenly on both halves of bread and sprinkle lightly with black pepper. Place halves together and cut loaf vertically into 8 equal pieces, being careful to keep loaf intact. Wrap tightly in foil. Bake 30 minutes.

4. To serve, unwrap loaf leaving foil crushed around outside to keep warm.
                                                    Makes 16 servings

Vegetable-Stuffed Baked Potatoes

**1 jar (16 ounces) RAGÚ® Cheese Creations!® Roasted Garlic
Parmesan Sauce or Double Cheddar Sauce**
1 bag (16 ounces) frozen assorted vegetables, cooked and drained
6 large baking potatoes, unpeeled and baked

In 2-quart saucepan, heat Ragú Cheese Creations! Sauce. Stir in vegetables; heat through.

Cut a lengthwise slice from top of each potato. Lightly mash pulp in each potato. Evenly spoon sauce mixture onto each potato. Sprinkle, if desired, with ground black pepper. *Makes 6 servings*

Fresh Vegetable Sauté

2 tablespoons olive oil
**6 cups assorted cut-up vegetables, such as broccoli flowerets, green
beans, cauliflowerets, sugar snap peas, bell pepper strips,
diagonally sliced carrots, mushrooms, onions, yellow squash
and zucchini**
1 envelope GOOD SEASONS® Italian Salad Dressing Mix
2 tablespoons red wine vinegar

HEAT oil in large skillet on medium-high heat. Add vegetables; cook and stir until tender-crisp.

ADD salad dressing mix and vinegar; cook and stir until heated through. Garnish with chopped fresh parsley, if desired.
Makes 4 to 6 servings

Prep Time: 15 minutes
Cook Time: 15 minutes

Vegetable-Stuffed Baked Potato

Velveeta® Ultimate Macaroni & Cheese

2 cups (8 ounces) elbow macaroni, uncooked
1 pound (16 ounces) VELVEETA® Pasteurized Prepared Cheese
     Product, cut up
½ cup milk
Dash pepper

1. Cook macaroni as directed on package; drain well. Return to same pan.

2. Add Velveeta, milk and pepper to same pan. Stir on low heat until Velveeta is melted. Serve immediately.   *Makes 4 to 6 servings*

Prep Time: 5 minutes
Cook Time: 15 minutes

quick tip

> *Macaroni & cheese is a great side dish to complete any meal. Try it with pork, beef or chicken.*

Velveeta® Ultimate
Macaroni & Cheese

Honey-Glazed Carrots and Parsnips

½ **pound carrots, thinly sliced**
½ **pound parsnips, peeled and thinly sliced**
¼ **cup chopped fresh parsley**
2 **tablespoons honey**
   Additional fresh parsley (optional)

Steam carrots and parsnips over simmering water in large saucepan 3 to 4 minutes or until crisp-tender. Rinse under cold running water; drain. Combine carrots, parsnips, parsley and honey in same saucepan. Cook over medium heat just until heated through. Garnish with additional parsley, if desired. Serve immediately.

Makes 6 (⅔-cup) servings

Peas with Cukes 'n' Dill

2 **pounds fresh peas***
2 **tablespoons butter or margarine**
½ **medium cucumber, halved, seeded and cut into ¼-inch slices**
1 **teaspoon dried dill weed**
   Salt and pepper
   Fresh dill, pineapple sage leaves and edible flowers, such as pansies, for garnish

*Or, substitute 1 (10-ounce) package frozen peas, thawed, for fresh peas.

1. To prepare peas, press each pea pod between thumbs and forefingers to open.

2. Push peas out with thumb into colander; discard pods. Rinse peas under running water. Drain well; set aside.

3. Heat butter in medium skillet over medium-high heat until melted and bubbly. Cook and stir peas and cucumber in hot butter 5 minutes or until vegetables are crisp-tender.

4. Stir in dill weed; season with salt and pepper to taste. Transfer to warm serving dish. Garnish, if desired. Serve immediately.

Makes 4 servings

Swiss Rosti Potatoes

4 large russet potatoes (about 6 ounces each)*
4 tablespoons butter or margarine
  Salt and pepper
  Cherry tomato wedges and fresh rosemary sprigs for garnish

*Prepare potatoes several hours or up to 1 day in advance.

1. Preheat oven to 400°F. To prepare potatoes, scrub with soft vegetable brush under running water; rinse well. Pierce each potato in several places with fork. Bake 1 hour or until fork-tender. Cool completely, then refrigerate.

2. When potatoes are cold, peel with paring knife. Grate potatoes by hand with large section of metal grater or use food processor with large grater disk.

3. Heat butter in 10-inch skillet over medium-high heat until melted and bubbly. Press grated potatoes evenly into skillet. (Do not stir or turn potatoes.) Season with salt and pepper to taste. Cook 10 to 12 minutes until golden brown.

4. Turn off heat; invert serving plate over skillet. Turn potatoes out onto plate. Garnish, if desired. Serve immediately.

Makes 4 servings

Satisfying Side Dishes

Oven-Roasted Vegetables

1½ pounds assorted cut-up fresh vegetables*
3 tablespoons I CAN'T BELIEVE IT'S NOT BUTTER!® Spread, melted
2 cloves garlic, finely chopped
1 tablespoon chopped fresh oregano leaves *or* 1 teaspoon dried
oregano leaves, crushed
Salt and ground black pepper to taste

*Use any combination of the following: zucchini, red, green or yellow bell peppers, Spanish or red onions, white or portobello mushrooms and carrots.

Preheat oven to 450°F.

In bottom of broiler pan, without rack, combine all ingredients. Roast 20 minutes or until vegetables are tender, stirring once.

Makes 4 servings

Oven-Roasted Vegetables

Roasted Idaho & Sweet Potatoes

1 envelope LIPTON® RECIPE SECRETS® Onion Soup Mix
2 medium all-purpose potatoes, peeled, if desired, and cut into
　　large chunks (about 1 pound)
2 medium sweet potatoes or yams, peeled, if desired, and cut into
　　large chunks (about 1 pound)
¼ cup olive or vegetable oil

1. Preheat oven to 425°F. In large plastic bag or bowl, combine all ingredients. Close bag and shake, or toss in bowl, until potatoes are evenly coated.

2. In 13×9-inch baking or roasting pan, arrange potatoes; discard bag.

3. Bake uncovered, stirring occasionally, 40 minutes or until potatoes are tender and golden.　　　　　　　　　　　*Makes 4 servings*

quick tip

Sweet potatoes are a wonderful (and often overlooked) health food—they're fat free, a good source of fiber and a great source of beta-carotene. They are also rich in potassium and vitamin C.

Roasted Idaho & Sweet Potatoes

Apple Blossom Mold

1½ cups boiling water
  1 package (8-serving size) *or* 2 packages (4-serving size each)
    JELL-O® Brand Lemon Flavor Gelatin
  2 cups cold apple juice
  1 cup diced red and green apples

STIR boiling water into gelatin in large bowl at least 2 minutes until completely dissolved. Stir in cold juice. Refrigerate about 1½ hours or until thickened (spoon drawn through leaves definite impression). Stir in apples. Pour into 6-cup mold which has been sprayed with no stick cooking spray.

REFRIGERATE 4 hours or until firm. Unmold. Garnish as desired.

Makes 10 servings

Variation: Sugar Free Low Calorie Gelatin may be substituted.

Prep Time: 15 minutes
Refrigerate Time: 5½ hours

Apple Blossom Mold

Satisfying Side Dishes

Tempting
POULTRY

Garlic Mushroom Chicken Melt

4 boneless, skinless chicken breast halves (about 1¼ pounds)
1 envelope LIPTON® RECIPE SECRETS® Savory Herb with Garlic Soup Mix
1 can (14 ounces) diced tomatoes, undrained *or* 1 large tomato, chopped
1 tablespoon olive or vegetable oil
½ cup shredded mozzarella or Monterey Jack cheese (about 2 ounces)

1. Preheat oven to 375°F. In 13×9-inch baking or roasting pan, arrange chicken. Pour soup mix blended with tomatoes and oil over chicken.

2. Bake, uncovered, 25 minutes or until chicken is no longer pink.

3. Sprinkle with mozzarella cheese and bake an additional 2 minutes or until cheese is melted.   *Makes 4 servings*

Garlic Mushroom Chicken Melt

Summer Raspberry Chicken

4 boneless, skinless chicken breast halves (about 1 pound), pounded to ¼-inch thickness

¾ cup LAWRY'S® Dijon & Honey Marinade with Lemon Juice, divided

1 cup fresh or frozen raspberries

½ cup walnut pieces

Grill or broil chicken 10 to 15 minutes or until no longer pink in center and juices run clear when cut, turning once and basting often with ½ cup Dijon & Honey Marinade. *Do not baste during last 5 minutes of cooking.* Discard any remaining marinade. Cut chicken into strips. In food processor or blender, process raspberries and additional ¼ cup Dijon & Honey Marinade 10 seconds. Drizzle raspberry sauce over chicken; sprinkle with walnuts. *Makes 4 servings*

quick tip

Serve chicken on field greens or angel hair pasta. Garnish with fresh raspberries, if desired.

Summer Raspberry Chicken

Classic Fried Chicken

¾ cup all-purpose flour
1 teaspoon salt
¼ teaspoon pepper
1 frying chicken (2½ to 3 pounds), cut up, or chicken pieces
½ cup CRISCO® Oil*

Use your favorite Crisco Oil product.

1. Combine flour, salt and pepper in paper or plastic bag. Add a few pieces of chicken at a time. Shake to coat.

2. Heat oil to 365°F in electric skillet or on medium-high heat in large heavy skillet. Fry chicken 30 to 40 minutes without lowering heat. Turn once for even browning. Drain on paper towels.   *Makes 4 servings*

Note: For thicker crust, increase flour to 1½ cups. Shake damp chicken in seasoned flour. Place on waxed paper. Let stand for 5 to 20 minutes before frying.

Spicy Fried Chicken: Increase pepper to ½ teaspoon. Combine pepper with ½ teaspoon poultry seasoning, ½ teaspoon paprika, ½ teaspoon cayenne pepper and ¼ teaspoon dry mustard. Rub on chicken before step 1. Substitute 2¼ teaspoons garlic salt, ¼ teaspoon salt and ¼ teaspoon celery salt for 1 teaspoon salt. Combine with flour in step 1 and proceed as directed above.

Classic Fried Chicken

Country Herb Roasted Chicken

1 chicken (2½ to 3 pounds), cut into serving pieces (with or without skin) *or* 1½ pounds boneless skinless chicken breast halves
1 envelope LIPTON® RECIPE SECRETS® Savory Herb with Garlic Soup Mix
2 tablespoons water
1 tablespoon BERTOLLI® Olive Oil

1. Preheat oven to 375°F.

2. In 13×9-inch baking or roasting pan, arrange chicken. In small bowl, combine remaining ingredients; brush on chicken.

3. For chicken pieces, bake uncovered 45 minutes or until chicken is no longer pink. For chicken breast halves, bake uncovered 20 minutes or until chicken is no longer pink. *Makes about 4 servings*

quick tip

> To make a complete meal, serve this dish with a lettuce and tomato salad, scalloped potatoes and cooked green beans.

Caribbean Jerk Chicken with Quick Fruit Salsa

1 cup plus 2 tablespoons LAWRY'S® Caribbean Jerk Marinade with Papaya Juice, divided
1 can (15¼ ounces) tropical fruit salad, drained
4 boneless, skinless chicken breast halves (about 1 pound)

In small glass bowl, combine 2 tablespoons Caribbean Jerk Marinade and tropical fruit; mix well and set aside. In large resealable plastic food storage bag, combine additional 1 cup Caribbean Jerk Marinade and chicken; seal bag. Marinate in refrigerator at least 30 minutes. Remove chicken from marinade; discard used marinade. Grill or broil chicken until no longer pink in center, about 10 to 15 minutes, turning halfway through grilling time. Top chicken with fruit salsa.

Makes 4 servings

Serving Suggestion: Serve with hot cooked rice and black beans.

Asian Chicken and Noodles

1 package (3 ounces) chicken flavor instant ramen noodles
1 bag (16 ounces) BIRDS EYE® frozen Farm Fresh Mixtures Broccoli, Carrots and Water Chestnuts*
1 tablespoon vegetable oil
1 pound boneless skinless chicken breasts, cut into thin strips
¼ cup stir-fry sauce

*Or, substitute 1 bag (16 ounces) Birds Eye® frozen Broccoli Cuts.

• Reserve seasoning packet from noodles.

• Bring 2 cups water to boil in large saucepan. Add noodles and vegetables. Cook 3 minutes, stirring occasionally; drain.

• Meanwhile, heat oil in large nonstick skillet over medium-high heat. Add chicken; cook and stir until browned, about 8 minutes.

• Stir in noodles, vegetables, stir-fry sauce and reserved seasoning packet; heat through.

Makes about 4 servings

Grilled Rosemary Chicken

2 tablespoons lemon juice
2 tablespoons olive oil
2 cloves garlic, minced
2 tablespoons minced fresh rosemary
¼ teaspoon salt
4 boneless skinless chicken breasts

1. Whisk together lemon juice, oil, garlic, rosemary and salt in small bowl. Pour into shallow glass dish. Add chicken, turning to coat both sides with lemon juice mixture. Cover and marinate in refrigerator 15 minutes, turning chicken once.

2. Grill chicken over medium-hot coals 5 to 6 minutes per side or until chicken is no longer pink in center. *Makes 4 servings*

Prep and Cook Time: 30 minutes

quick tip

For added flavor, moisten a few sprigs of fresh rosemary and toss on the hot coals just before grilling.

Grilled Rosemary Chicken

Wish-Bone® Marinade Italiano

¾ cup WISH-BONE® Italian Dressing*
2½ to 3 pounds chicken pieces

*Also terrific with Wish-Bone® Robusto Italian or Just 2 Good Italian Dressing.

In large, shallow nonaluminum baking dish or plastic bag, pour ½ cup Italian dressing over chicken. Cover, or close bag, and marinate in refrigerator, turning occasionally, 3 to 24 hours.

Remove chicken from marinade; discard marinade. Grill or broil chicken, turning once and brushing frequently with remaining ¼ cup dressing, until chicken is no longer pink and juices run clear.

Makes about 4 servings

quick tip

One (2- to 2½-pound) T-bone, boneless sirloin or top loin steak or 6 boneless, skinless chicken breast halves (about 1½ pounds) or 2½ pounds center cut pork chops (about 1 inch thick) may be substituted for chicken pieces.

Wish-Bone® Marinade Italiano

Velveeta® Cheesy Chicken & Rice Skillet

1 tablespoon oil
4 small boneless skinless chicken breast halves (about 1 pound)
1 can (10¾ ounces) condensed cream of chicken soup
1 soup can (1⅓ cups) water
2 cups MINUTE® White Rice, uncooked
**1 package (8 ounces) VELVEETA® Shredded Pasteurized Process
  Cheese Food, divided**

1. Heat oil in large nonstick skillet on medium-high heat. Add chicken; cover. Cook 4 minutes on each side or until cooked through. Remove chicken from skillet.

2. Add soup and water to skillet; stir. Bring to boil.

3. Stir in rice and 1 cup of the Velveeta. Top with chicken. Sprinkle with remaining Velveeta; cover. Cook on low heat 5 minutes.

Makes 4 servings

Note: Increase oil to 2 tablespoons if using regular skillet.

Tip: A general rule for chicken doneness is when the juices run clear and the meat is no longer pink. If you use a thermometer, the internal temperature in the thickest part of the chicken breast should reach 170°F.

Prep Time: 5 minutes
Cook Time: 15 minutes

Velveeta® Cheesy Chicken &
Rice Skillet

Cajun Chicken Bayou

2 cups water
1 can (10 ounces) diced tomatoes and green chilies, undrained
1 box UNCLE BEN'S CHEF'S RECIPE™ Traditional Red Beans & Rice
3 TYSON® Individually Fresh Frozen® Boneless, Skinless Chicken
Breasts

COOK: CLEAN: Wash hands. In large skillet, combine water, tomatoes, beans and rice, and contents of seasoning packet; mix well. Add chicken. Bring to a boil. Cover, reduce heat; simmer 30 to 35 minutes or until internal juices of chicken run clear. (Or insert instant-read meat thermometer in thickest part of chicken. Temperature should read 170°F.)

SERVE: Serve with sliced avocados and whole wheat rolls, if desired.

CHILL: Refrigerate leftovers immediately.   *Makes 3 servings*

Prep Time: none
Cook Time: 35 minutes

Herbed Chicken & Vegetables

2 medium all-purpose potatoes, thinly sliced (about 1 pound)
2 medium carrots, sliced
4 bone-in chicken pieces (about 2 pounds)
1 envelope LIPTON® RECIPE SECRETS® Savory Herb with Garlic
    Soup Mix
⅓ cup water
1 tablespoon olive or vegetable oil

1. Preheat oven to 425°F. In broiler pan, without the rack, place potatoes and carrots; arrange chicken on top. Pour soup mix blended with water and oil over chicken and vegetables.

2. Bake uncovered 40 minutes or until chicken is no longer pink and vegetables are tender.   *Makes 4 servings*

Slow Cooker Method: Place all ingredients in slow cooker, arranging chicken on top; cover. Cook on HIGH 4 hours or LOW 6 to 8 hours.

Prep Time: 10 minutes
Cook Time: 40 minutes

Tender Baked Chicken

1 chicken (2½ to 3½ pounds), cut into pieces
½ cup HELLMANN'S® or BEST FOODS® Real or Light Mayonnaise
1¼ cups Italian seasoned bread crumbs

1. Brush chicken on all sides with mayonnaise.

2. Place bread crumbs in large plastic food storage bag. Add chicken 1 piece at a time; shake to coat well. Arrange on rack in broiler pan.

3. Bake in 425°F oven about 40 minutes or until golden brown and tender. *Makes 4 servings*

Di Giorno® Easy Chicken Cacciatore with Light Ravioli

1 package (9 ounces) DI GIORNO® Light Cheese Ravioli
2 boneless skinless chicken breast halves, cut into strips
1 large green pepper, thinly sliced
1 package (15 ounces) DI GIORNO® Marinara Sauce

PREPARE pasta as directed on package.

MEANWHILE, spray large nonstick skillet with no stick cooking spray. Add chicken; cook and stir on medium-high heat until cooked through. Add green pepper; cook and stir 1 minute.

STIR in sauce; cook on low heat 1 minute or until thoroughly heated. Toss with pasta. Sprinkle with DI GIORNO Shredded Parmesan Cheese, if desired. *Makes 4 servings*

Prep Time: 5 minutes
Cook Time: 10 minutes

Tender Baked Chicken

Roasted Chicken au Jus

1 envelope LIPTON® RECIPE SECRETS® Garlic Mushroom Soup Mix*
2 tablespoons olive or vegetable oil
1 (2½- to 3-pound) chicken, cut into serving pieces
½ cup hot water

*Also terrific with LIPTON® RECIPE SECRETS® Savory Herb with Garlic Soup Mix.

1. Preheat oven to 425°F. In large bowl, combine soup mix and oil; add chicken and toss until evenly coated.

2. In bottom of broiler pan without rack, arrange chicken. Roast chicken, basting occasionally, 40 minutes or until chicken is no longer pink.

3. Remove chicken to serving platter. Add hot water to pan and stir, scraping brown bits from bottom of pan. Serve sauce over chicken.

Makes 4 servings

Roasted Chicken au Jus

Crispy Ranch Chicken

1½ cups cornflake crumbs
1 teaspoon dried rosemary
½ teaspoon salt
½ teaspoon black pepper
1½ cups ranch salad dressing
3 pounds chicken pieces (breasts, legs, thighs)

Preheat oven to 375°F. Combine cornflakes, rosemary, salt and pepper in medium bowl.

Pour salad dressing in separate medium bowl. Dip chicken pieces in salad dressing, coating well. Dredge coated chicken in crumb mixture.

Place in 13×9-inch baking dish coated with nonstick cooking spray. Bake 50 to 55 minutes or until juices run clear. Serve with desired side dishes. *Makes 6 servings*

quick tip

To add an Italian flare to this dish, try substituting 1½ cups Italian-seasoned dried bread crumbs and ½ cup grated Parmesan cheese for the cornflake crumbs, rosemary, salt and pepper. Prepare recipe as directed.

Crispy Ranch Chicken

One-Dish Meal

2 bags SUCCESS® Rice
   Vegetable cooking spray
1 cup cubed cooked turkey-ham*
1 cup (4 ounces) shredded low-fat Cheddar cheese
1 cup peas

Or, use cooked turkey, ham or turkey franks.

Prepare rice according to package directions.

Spray 1-quart microwave-safe dish with cooking spray; set aside. Place rice in medium bowl. Add ham, cheese and peas; mix lightly. Spoon into prepared dish; smooth into even layer with spoon. Microwave on HIGH 1 minute; stir. Microwave 30 seconds or until thoroughly heated.

Makes 4 servings

Conventional Oven Directions: Assemble casserole as directed. Spoon into ovenproof 1-quart baking dish sprayed with vegetable cooking spray. Bake at 350°F until thoroughly heated, about 15 to 20 minutes.

One-Dish Meal

Peppery Turkey Fillets

1 package (about ¾ pound) PERDUE® FIT 'N EASY® Fresh Skinless & Boneless Turkey Breast Fillets
¼ cup Worcestershire sauce
1 tablespoon Dijon mustard
1 tablespoon canola oil
2 teaspoons cracked black pepper
Salt

Place fillets in shallow baking dish. In small bowl, combine Worcestershire sauce, mustard and oil. Add fillets to marinade, turning to coat well. Cover and refrigerate 1 hour or longer.

Prepare lightly greased grill for cooking. Remove fillets from marinade; sprinkle with pepper and salt to taste. Grill, uncovered, 5 to 6 inches over medium-hot coals 3 to 5 minutes on each side until cooked through. *Makes 3 to 4 servings*

quick tip

If possible, use a pepper grinder or mortar and pestle to grind pepper as you need it for cooking—the taste is far superior to that of preground pepper, which loses its flavor very quickly.

Roast Stuffed Turkey

2 packages (6 ounces each) STOVE TOP® Stuffing Mix, any variety
½ cup (1 stick) butter or margarine, cut into pieces
3 cups hot water
1 (8- to 10-pound) turkey

Prepare stuffing by placing contents of vegetable/seasoning packets and butter in large bowl. Add hot water; stir just to partially melt butter. Add stuffing crumbs. Stir just to moisten. Do not stuff bird until ready to roast.

Rinse turkey with cold water; pat dry. Do not rub cavity with salt. Lightly stuff neck and body cavities with prepared stuffing. Skewer neck skin to back. Tie legs to tail and twist wing tips under. Place turkey, breast side up, in roasting pan. Roast at 325°F for 3 to 4 hours or as directed on poultry wrapper. Bake any remaining stuffing in greased baking dish at 325°F for 30 minutes. Cover for moist stuffing. If drier stuffing is desired, bake uncovered.

Makes 8 to 10 servings

Cutlets Milanese

1 package (about 1 pound) PERDUE® FIT 'N EASY® Fresh Thin-Sliced
Turkey or Chicken Breast Cutlets
Salt and ground pepper to taste
½ cup Italian seasoned bread crumbs
½ cup grated Parmesan cheese
1 large egg beaten with 1 teaspoon water
2 to 3 tablespoons olive oil

Season cutlets with salt and pepper. On wax paper, combine bread crumbs and Parmesan cheese. Dip cutlets in egg mixture and roll in bread crumb mixture. In large, nonstick skillet over medium-high heat, heat oil. Add cutlets and sauté 3 minutes per side, until golden brown and cooked through.

Makes 4 servings

Prep Time: 6 to 8 minutes
Cook Time: 6 minutes

Grilled Turkey with Roasted Garlic Grilled Corn

1 (4½- to 9-pound) Li'l BUTTERBALL® Young Turkey, thawed, giblets
    removed
Vegetable oil
8 ears fresh corn in husks
1 whole bulb fresh garlic
Olive oil

Prepare charcoal covered grill for indirect-heat cooking. Position foil drip pan in middle of bottom rack; place 25 to 30 briquettes along the outside of each lengthwise side of the drip pan. Burn briquettes until covered with gray ash, about 30 minutes. Place top rack in grill with handle openings over coals.

Turn wings back to hold neck skin in place. Return legs to tucked position if untucked. Brush turkey with vegetable oil to prevent skin from drying. Insert meat thermometer into thickest part of thigh not touching bone.

Place unstuffed turkey, breast up, in center of rack over drip pan. Cover grill and leave vents open. Add 6 to 8 briquettes to each side every hour or as needed to maintain heat. Cook turkey to an internal thigh temperature of 180°F and breast to 170°F. (A 4½- to 9-pound turkey will take about 1½ to 2½ hours.)

To prepare corn and garlic for grilling, leave corn in husks and soak in cold water for 30 minutes. Carefully pull back husks and remove silks, leaving husks attached. Smooth husks over corn to enclose. Cut ½ inch off tip of garlic bulb; drizzle garlic with olive oil and wrap tightly in foil. Place corn and garlic on grill for last 30 to 40 minutes of grilling.

Remove husks and serve corn; spread with melted butter and roasted garlic. *Makes 8 servings*

Prep Time: 30 minutes plus grilling time

Grilled Turkey with Roasted Garlic
Grilled Corn

Butterflied Cornish Game Hens

2 Cornish game hens* (about 3 pounds)
Olive oil vegetable cooking spray
Seasoned salt
Ground black pepper
½ cup *French's*® Dijon Mustard
Grilled vegetables (optional)

*You may substitute 3 pounds chicken parts (skinned, if desired) for the game hens.

Remove neck and giblets from hens; discard. Wash hens and pat dry. Place 1 hen, breast side down, on cutting board. With kitchen shears or sharp knife, cut along one side of backbone, cutting as close to bone as possible. Cut down other side of backbone; remove backbone. Spread bird open and turn breast side up, pressing to flatten. Repeat with remaining hen.

To keep drumsticks flat, make small slit through skin with point of knife between thigh and breast. Push end of leg through slit. Repeat on other side of bird and with remaining hen. Coat both sides of hens with vegetable cooking spray. Sprinkle with seasoned salt and pepper. Generously brush mustard onto both sides of hens.

Place hens, skin sides up, on oiled grid. Grill over medium-high coals 35 to 45 minutes until meat is no longer pink near bone and juices run clear, turning and basting often with remaining mustard. (Do not baste during last 10 minutes of cooking.) Serve with grilled vegetables, if desired.   *Makes 4 servings*

Prep Time: 15 minutes
Cook Time: 45 minutes

Butterflied Cornish Game Hens

Enticing
BEEF

Zesty Peppered Steaks

4 ounces PHILADELPHIA® Neufchâtel Cheese, ⅓ Less Fat Than Cream Cheese
½ cup A.1.® Original or A.1.® BOLD & SPICY Steak Sauce, divided
1 tablespoon prepared horseradish
4 (4-ounce) beef rib eye steaks, about ¾ inch thick
2 teaspoons coarsely ground black pepper

1. Heat cream cheese, ¼ cup steak sauce and horseradish in small saucepan, over medium heat until heated through; keep warm.

2. Brush both sides of steaks with 2 tablespoons steak sauce, dividing evenly. Sprinkle ¼ teaspoon pepper on each side of each steak, pressing into meat and sauce.

3. Grill steaks over medium-high heat or broil 4 inches from heat source 4 minutes on each side or to desired doneness, basting occasionally with remaining 2 tablespoons steak sauce. Serve with warm sauce. Garnish as desired.   *Makes 4 servings*

Zesty Peppered Steak

Prime Rib

3 cloves garlic, minced
1 teaspoon black pepper
1 (3-rib) standing beef roast, trimmed* (about 6 to 7 pounds)

*Ask meat retailer to remove chine bone for easier carving. Fat should be trimmed to ¼-inch thickness.

1. Preheat oven to 450°F.

2. Combine garlic and pepper; rub over all surfaces of roast. Place roast, bone side down, in shallow roasting pan. Insert meat thermometer into thickest part of roast not touching bone or fat.

3. Roast in oven 15 minutes. *Reduce oven temperature to 325°F.* Roast 20 minutes per pound for medium or until internal temperature reaches 145°F when tested with meat thermometer inserted into thickest part of roast, not touching bone. Transfer roast to cutting board; cover with foil.

4. Let stand 15 to 20 minutes to allow for easier carving. Internal temperature will continue to rise 5° to 10°F during stand time. Carve; serve immediately. Garnish as desired.   *Makes 6 to 8 servings*

Souper Stuffed Cheese Burgers

1 envelope LIPTON® RECIPE SECRETS® Onion Soup Mix*
2 pounds ground beef
½ cup water
¾ cup shredded Cheddar, mozzarella or Monterey Jack cheese
(about 6 ounces)

*Also terrific with LIPTON® RECIPE SECRETS® Savory Herb with Garlic, Onion-Mushroom or Beefy Onion Soup Mix.

1. In large bowl, combine soup mix, ground beef and water; shape into 12 patties.

2. Place 2 tablespoons cheese in center of 6 patties. Top with remaining patties and seal edges tightly.

3. Grill or broil until done. Serve, if desired, on onion poppy seed rolls.   *Makes 6 servings*

quick tip

> To perk up your burgers, serve them on something
> besides a bun. Try bagels, English muffins, pita bread or
> even tortillas for a fun change of pace!

Velveeta® Beef Enchiladas Olé

1 pound ground beef or 1 pound boneless skinless chicken breasts, chopped

1 cup TACO BELL® HOME ORIGINALS®* Thick 'N Chunky Salsa, divided

1 pound (16 ounces) VELVEETA® Mexican Pasteurized Process Cheese Spread with Jalapeño Peppers, cut up, divided

10 flour tortillas

*TACO BELL and HOME ORIGINALS are registered trademarks owned and licensed by Taco Bell Corp.

1. Brown meat; drain. Stir in ½ cup of the salsa and ½ of the Velveeta; cook and stir on medium-low heat until Velveeta is melted.

2. Spoon ¼ cup meat mixture in center of each tortilla; roll up. Place tortillas, seam side down, in microwavable baking dish. Top with remaining ½ cup salsa and Velveeta. Cover loosely with microwavable plastic wrap.

3. Microwave on HIGH 4 to 6 minutes or until Velveeta is melted.

Makes 5 servings

Tip: Flour tortillas come in many colors and sizes. You'll find them in the refrigerated dairy case or grocery aisle of the supermarket. You'll also find tortillas in a variety of flavors such as herb, tomato or spinach, all of which can be used in Beef Enchiladas Olé.

Prep Time: 20 minutes
Microwave Time: 6 minutes

Velveeta® Beef Enchiladas Olé

Cheesy Spinach Burgers

1 envelope LIPTON® RECIPE SECRETS® Onion Soup Mix
2 pounds ground beef
1 package (10 ounces) frozen chopped spinach, thawed and
**   squeezed dry**
1 cup shredded mozzarella or Cheddar cheese (about 4 ounces)

1. In large bowl, combine all ingredients; shape into 8 patties.

2. Grill or broil until done. Serve, if desired, on hamburger buns.

Makes 8 servings

quick tip

> Serve these tasty burgers with your favorite side dish.
> Make your own French fries or potato chips, or choose
> ready-made brands.

Cheesy Spinach Burgers

Beefy Mac & Double Cheddar

½ pound ground beef
3½ cups water
2 cups elbow macaroni
1 jar (16 ounces) RAGÚ® Cheese Creations!® Double Cheddar Sauce

In 12-inch skillet, brown ground beef; drain. Remove from skillet and set aside.

In same skillet, bring water to a boil over high heat. Stir in macaroni and cook 6 minutes or until tender; do not drain. Return ground beef to skillet. Stir in Ragú Cheese Creations! Sauce; heat through. Season, if desired, with salt and ground black pepper.   *Makes 4 servings*

Cheeseburger Soup

½ **pound ground beef**
3½ **cups water**
½ **cup cherry tomato halves or chopped tomato**
1 **pouch LIPTON® Soup Secrets Ring-O-Noodle Soup Mix with Real Chicken Broth**
4 **ounces Cheddar cheese, shredded**

Shape ground beef into 16 mini burgers.

In large saucepan, thoroughly brown burgers; drain. Add water, tomatoes and soup mix; bring to a boil. Reduce heat and simmer uncovered, stirring occasionally, 5 minutes or until burgers are cooked and noodles are tender. Stir in cheese.

Makes about 4 (1-cup) servings

93

Fragrant Beef with Garlic Sauce

1 boneless beef top sirloin steak, cut 1 inch thick (about
    1¼ pounds)
⅓ cup reduced-sodium teriyaki sauce
10 large cloves garlic, peeled
½ cup defatted reduced-sodium beef broth
4 cups hot cooked white rice (optional)

1. Place beef in large plastic bag. Pour teriyaki sauce over beef. Close bag securely; turn to coat. Marinate in refrigerator at least 30 minutes or up to 4 hours.

2. Combine garlic and broth in small saucepan. Bring to a boil over high heat. Reduce heat to medium. Simmer, uncovered, 5 minutes. Cover and simmer 8 to 9 minutes until garlic is softened. Transfer to blender or food processor; process until smooth.

3. Meanwhile, drain beef; reserve marinade. Place beef on rack of broiler pan. Brush with half of reserved marinade. Broil 5 to 6 inches from heat 5 minutes. Turn beef over; brush with remaining marinade. Broil 5 minutes more.*

4. Slice beef thinly; serve with garlic sauce and rice, if desired.

Makes 4 servings

*Broiling time is for medium-rare doneness. Adjust time for desired doneness.

Fragrant Beef with Garlic Sauce

Marinated Flank Steak with Pineapple

1 can (15¼ ounces) DEL MONTE® Sliced Pineapple In Its Own Juice
¼ cup teriyaki sauce
2 tablespoons honey
1 pound flank steak

1. Drain pineapple, reserving 2 tablespoons juice. Set aside pineapple for later use.

2. Combine reserved juice, teriyaki sauce and honey in shallow 2-quart dish; mix well. Add meat; turn to coat. Cover and refrigerate at least 30 minutes or overnight.

3. Remove meat from marinade, reserving marinade. Grill meat over hot coals (or broil), brushing occasionally with reserved marinade. Cook about 4 minutes on each side for rare, about 5 minutes on each side for medium, or about 6 minutes on each side for well done. During last 4 minutes of cooking, brush pineapple slices with marinade; grill until heated through.

4. Slice meat across grain; serve with pineapple. Garnish, if desired.

Makes 4 servings

Note: Marinade that has come into contact with raw meat must be discarded or boiled for several minutes before serving with cooked food.

Prep and Marinate Time: 35 minutes
Cook Time: 10 minutes

Marinated Flank Steak with Pineapple

Velveeta® Salsa Mac

1 pound ground beef
1 jar (16 ounces) TACO BELL® HOME ORIGINALS®* Thick 'N Chunky
   Salsa
1¾ cups water
 2 cups (8 ounces) elbow macaroni, uncooked
 ¾ pound (12 ounces) VELVEETA® Pasteurized Prepared Cheese
    Product, cut up

*TACO BELL and HOME ORIGINALS are registered trademarks owned and licensed by Taco Bell Corp.

1. Brown meat in large skillet; drain.

2. Stir in salsa and water. Bring to boil. Stir in macaroni. Reduce heat to medium-low; cover. Simmer 8 to 10 minutes or until macaroni is tender.

3. Add Velveeta; stir until melted.   *Makes 4 to 6 servings*

Spicy Substitute: For an extra spicy kick in Salsa Mac, try making it with Velveeta Mild or Hot Mexican Pasteurized Process Cheese Spread with Jalapeño Peppers. Be careful though...the hot is really hot!

Prep Time: 10 minutes
Cook Time: 15 minutes

Velveeta® Salsa Mac

Ultimate The Original Ranch® Cheese Burgers

1 packet (1 ounce) HIDDEN VALLEY® The Original Ranch® Seasoning & Salad Dressing Mix
1 pound ground beef
1 cup (4 ounces) shredded Cheddar cheese
4 large hamburger buns, toasted

Combine dressing mix with beef and cheese. Shape into 4 patties; cook thoroughly until no longer pink in center. Serve on toasted buns.

Makes 4 servings

quick tip

Grilling is a great way to cook these burgers. To minimize food sticking to the grid and to assist in the cleanup, grease grill grid with oil or cooking spray before use. However, do not spray the grid over the fire as this could cause a flare-up.

Stir-Fried Beef & Spinach

Nonstick cooking spray
5 ounces fresh spinach leaves, torn
Dash salt
8 ounces top sirloin steak, thinly sliced
¼ cup stir-fry sauce
1 teaspoon sugar
½ teaspoon curry powder
¼ teaspoon ground ginger

1. Coat 12-inch nonstick skillet with cooking spray. Heat skillet over high heat until hot. Add spinach; stir-fry 1 minute or until limp.

2. Remove skillet from heat; transfer spinach to serving platter, sprinkle with salt and cover to keep warm.

3. Wipe out skillet with paper towel. Coat skillet with cooking spray. Heat over high heat until hot. Add beef; stir-fry 1 minute until no longer pink. Add sauce, sugar, curry powder and ginger; cook and stir 1½ minutes or until sauce thickly coats beef.

4. Spoon beef mixture onto spinach.   *Makes 2 servings*

Steakhouse London Broil

1 package KNORR® Recipe Classics™ Roasted Garlic Herb or French Onion Soup, Dip and Recipe Mix
⅓ cup vegetable or olive oil
2 tablespoons red wine vinegar
1 (1½- to 2-pound) beef round steak (for London Broil) or flank steak

• In large plastic food bag or 13×9-inch glass baking dish, blend recipe mix, oil and vinegar.

• Add steak, turning to coat. Close bag, or cover, and marinate in refrigerator 30 minutes to 3 hours.

• Remove meat from marinade, discarding marinade. Grill or broil, turning occasionally, until desired doneness.

• Slice meat thinly across the grain.   *Makes 6 to 8 servings*

Prep Time: 5 minutes
Marinate Time: 30 minutes to 3 hours
Grill Time: 20 minutes

Steakhouse London Broil and Onion-
Roasted Potatoes (page 30)

Skillet Pasta Dinner

    und ground beef
   jar (26 to 28 ounces) RAGÚ® Robusto! Pasta Sauce
   8 ounces rotini pasta, cooked and drained
   1 cup shredded cheddar or Monterey Jack cheese, divided
   2 teaspoons chili powder (optional)

In 12-inch skillet, brown ground beef over medium-high heat; drain.
Stir in Ragú® Hearty Robust Blend Pasta Sauce, hot pasta, ¾ cup cheese
and chili powder. Simmer uncovered, stirring occasionally, 5 minutes or
until heated through. Sprinkle with remaining ¼ cup cheese.

Makes 4 servings

Grilled Sauerbraten Steak

½ **cup A.1.® Steak Sauce**
½ **cup dry red wine**
 1 **(1½-pound) boneless beef sirloin steak**
½ **cup water**
 2 **tablespoons margarine or butter**
 2 **gingersnap cookies, finely rolled**

Blend steak sauce and wine. Place steak in glass dish; coat with ½ cup steak sauce mixture. Cover; refrigerate 1 hour, turning occasionally.

Heat remaining steak sauce mixture, water, margarine and cookie crumbs to a boil in small saucepan over medium heat. Reduce heat and simmer 2 to 3 minutes or until thickened; keep warm.

Remove steak from marinade, discard marinade. Grill over medium heat for 15 to 20 minutes or until done, turning once. Slice steak and serve with warm sauce. *Makes 6 servings*

Blue Cheese Burgers

1¼ pounds lean ground beef
1 tablespoon finely chopped onion
**1½ teaspoons chopped fresh thyme _or_ ½ teaspoon dried thyme
    leaves**
¾ teaspoon salt
  Dash ground pepper
4 ounces blue cheese, crumbled

Preheat grill.

Combine ground beef, onion, thyme, salt and pepper in medium
bowl; mix lightly. Shape into eight patties.

Place cheese in center of four patties to within ½ inch of outer edge;
top with remaining burgers. Press edges together to seal.

Grill 8 minutes or to desired doneness, turning once. Serve with
lettuce, tomatoes and Dijon mustard on whole wheat buns, if desired.

Makes 4 servings

Blue Cheese Burger

Phenomenal

PORK

Grilled Sherry Pork Chops

¼ cup HOLLAND HOUSE® Sherry Cooking Wine
¼ cup GRANDMA'S® Molasses
2 tablespoons soy sauce
4 pork chops (1 inch thick)

In plastic bowl, combine sherry, molasses and soy sauce; pour over pork chops. Cover; refrigerate 30 minutes. Prepare grill. Drain pork chops; save marinade. Grill pork chops over medium-high heat 20 to 30 minutes or until pork is no longer pink in center, turning once and brushing frequently with marinade.* Discard any remaining marinade. *Makes 4 servings*

Do not baste during last 5 minutes of grilling.

Grilled Sherry Pork Chop

Hickory Pork Tenderloin
with Apple Topping

1¼ cups plus 2 tablespoons LAWRY'S® Hickory Marinade with Apple Cider, divided
1 pork tenderloin (2½ to 3 pounds)
1 can (21 ounces) apple pie filling or topping

In large resealable plastic food storage bag, combine 1 cup Hickory Marinade and tenderloin; seal bag. Marinate in refrigerator at least 30 minutes. Remove tenderloin from marinade; discard used marinade. Grill tenderloin, using indirect heat method, until no longer pink, about 35 minutes, turning once and basting often with additional ¼ cup Hickory Marinade. Let stand 10 minutes before slicing. In medium saucepan, combine additional 2 tablespoons Hickory Marinade and apple pie filling. Cook over low heat until heated throughout. Spoon over tenderloin slices.

Makes 6 to 8 servings

Serving Suggestion: Serve with brussels sprouts and cornbread. Garnish with cranberries, if desired.

Hint: Various flavored applesauces can be substituted for the apple pie filling. Try chunky applesauce with brown sugar and cinnamon.

Hickory Pork Tenderloin
with Apple Topping

Velveeta® 15 Minute Cheesy Rice with Ham & Broccoli

2 cups cooked ham cut into strips
2 cups fresh or frozen broccoli flowerets, thawed
1 cup water
1½ cups MINUTE® White Rice, uncooked
**½ pound (8 ounces) VELVEETA® Pasteurized Prepared Cheese
   Product, cut up**

1. Bring ham, broccoli and water to boil in large skillet. Cover. Cook on medium heat 3 minutes.

2. Stir in rice and Velveeta; cover. Remove from heat. Let stand 7 minutes. Stir until Velveeta is melted.   *Makes 4 servings*

Lean Homemade Sausage

1 pound lean ground pork
½ teaspoon ground rosemary
⅛ teaspoon salt
⅛ teaspoon ground thyme
⅛ teaspoon dried marjoram, crushed
⅛ teaspoon pepper

Combine all ingredients; mix well. Place in an air-tight container. Refrigerate 4 to 24 hours to allow flavors to blend.

Shape into ½-inch-thick patties. Cook patties in large skillet over medium heat 4 to 5 minutes on each side or until done. Or, place patties on unheated rack in broiler pan. Broil 5 inches from heat about 5 minutes on each side. *Makes 8 servings*

Prep Time: 10 minutes
Cook Time: 10 minutes

*Favorite recipe from **National Pork Board***

Peachy Pork Picante

4 boneless top loin pork chops, cubed
2 tablespoons taco seasoning
1 cup salsa
4 tablespoons peach preserves

Toss pork with taco seasoning. Lightly brown pork in a nonstick skillet over medium-high heat; stir in salsa and preserves. Bring to a boil, lower heat. Cover and simmer 8 to 10 minutes.   *Makes 4 servings*

Favorite recipe from **National Pork Board**

Peppered Pork Tenderloin

1 pork tenderloin, about 1 pound
2 teaspoons lemon pepper
½ teaspoon cayenne (red pepper) or pepper blend seasoning

Rub tenderloin all over with combined peppers; place in shallow roasting pan and roast in 425°F oven for 15 to 20 minutes, until internal temperature (measured with a meat thermometer) reads 155° to 160°F. Let roast rest for 5 minutes before slicing.
Makes 4 servings

Favorite recipe from **National Pork Board**

Peachy Pork Picante

Onion-Baked Pork Chops

1 envelope LIPTON® RECIPE SECRETS® Golden Onion Soup Mix*
⅓ cup plain dry bread crumbs
4 pork chops, 1 inch thick (about 3 pounds)
1 egg, well beaten

*Also terrific with LIPTON® RECIPE SECRETS® Onion or Savory Herb with Garlic Soup Mix.

1. Preheat oven to 400°F. In small bowl, combine soup mix and bread crumbs. Dip chops in egg, then bread crumb mixture, until evenly coated.

2. In lightly greased 13×9-inch baking or roasting pan, arrange chops.

3. Bake uncovered 20 minutes or until barely pink in center, turning once. *Makes 4 servings*

quick tip

> Serve this dish with a side of steamed vegetables, such as zucchini or carrots.

Onion-Baked Pork Chop

Lemon-Capered Pork Tenderloin

1½ pounds boneless pork tenderloin
1 tablespoon crushed capers
1 teaspoon dried rosemary
⅛ teaspoon black pepper
1 cup water
¼ cup lemon juice

1. Preheat oven to 350°F. Trim fat from tenderloin; discard. Set tenderloin aside.

2. Combine capers, rosemary and black pepper in small bowl. Rub rosemary mixture over tenderloin. Place tenderloin in shallow roasting pan. Pour water and lemon juice over tenderloin.

3. Bake, uncovered, 1 hour or until thermometer inserted in thickest part of tenderloin registers 170°F. Remove from oven; cover with foil. Allow to stand 10 minutes before serving. Garnish as desired.

Makes 8 servings

Lemon-Capered Pork Tenderloin

Barbecue Pork Skillet

4 top loin pork chops
¼ cup low-fat Italian dressing
¼ cup barbecue sauce
1 teaspoon chili powder

In large nonstick skillet, brown pork chops on one side over medium-high heat. Turn chops and add remaining ingredients to pan, stirring to blend. Cover and simmer for 5 to 8 minutes. *Makes 4 servings*

Favorite recipe from **National Pork Board**

Cure 81® Ham with Honey Mustard Glaze

1 CURE 81® half ham
1 cup packed brown sugar
½ cup honey
2 tablespoons prepared mustard

Bake ham according to package directions. Meanwhile, combine brown sugar, honey and mustard. Thirty minutes before ham is done, remove from oven. Score surface; spoon on glaze. Return to oven. Continue basting with glaze during last 30 minutes of baking.
Makes 8 to 10 servings

Garlic Pork Chops

6 bone-in pork chops, ¾ inch thick
1 envelope LIPTON® RECIPE SECRETS® Savory Herb with Garlic
    Soup Mix
2 tablespoons vegetable oil
½ cup hot water

1. Preheat oven to 425°F. In broiler pan, without the rack, arrange chops. Brush both sides of chops with soup mix combined with oil.

2. Bake chops 25 minutes or until barely pink in center.

3. Remove chops to serving platter. Add hot water to pan and stir, scraping brown bits from bottom of pan. Serve sauce over chops.

Makes 4 servings

Prep Time: 5 minutes
Cook Time: 25 minutes

Orange Mustard Ham Kabobs

¾ cup honey mustard barbecue sauce
½ cup orange marmalade
1½ pounds CURE 81® ham, cut into 1-inch cubes
2 small oranges, cut into 6 wedges each

In small bowl, combine barbecue sauce and marmalade; mix well. Remove ½ cup mixture for basting; reserve remaining mixture. Thread ham and orange wedges on skewers. Brush with ½ cup barbecue sauce mixture reserved for basting. Grill over medium-hot coals 10 minutes or until browned, turning frequently and basting with remaining barbecue mixture. Serve with reserved sauce mixture.

Makes 6 servings

quick tip

> *Orange Mustard Ham Kabobs may be broiled 6 inches from heat source for 10 minutes or until browned.*

Orange Mustard Ham Kabob

Pork Chops with Balsamic Vinegar

2 boneless center pork loin chops, 1½ inch thick
1½ teaspoons lemon pepper
1 teaspoon vegetable oil
3 tablespoons balsamic vinegar
2 tablespoons chicken broth
2 teaspoons butter

Pat chops dry. Coat with lemon pepper. Heat oil in heavy skillet over medium-high heat. Add chops. Brown on first side 8 minutes; turn and cook 7 minutes more or until done. Remove from pan and keep warm. Add vinegar and broth to skillet; cook, stirring, until syrupy (about 1 to 2 minutes). Stir in butter until blended. Spoon sauce over chops.

Makes 2 servings

Prep Time: 20 minutes

Favorite recipe from **National Pork Board**

Pork Chop with Balsamic Vinegar

Marinated Pork Roast

½ cup GRANDMA'S® Molasses
½ cup Dijon mustard
¼ cup tarragon vinegar
   Boneless pork loin roast (3 to 4 pounds)

1. In large plastic bowl, combine molasses, mustard and tarragon vinegar; mix well. Add pork to molasses mixture, turning to coat all sides. Marinate, covered, 1 to 2 hours at room temperature or overnight in refrigerator, turning several times.

2. Heat oven to 325°F. Remove pork from marinade; reserve marinade. Place pork in shallow roasting pan. Cook for 1 to 2 hours or until meat thermometer inserted into thickest part of roast reaches 160°F, basting with marinade* every 30 minutes; discard remaining marinade. Slice roast and garnish, if desired.

Makes 6 to 8 servings

*Do not baste during last 5 minutes of cooking.

Marinated Pork Roast

Pleasing
FISH & SHELLFISH

Hidden Valley® Broiled Fish

1 packet (1 ounce) HIDDEN VALLEY® The Original Ranch®
   Salad Dressing & Seasoning Mix
⅓ cup lemon juice
3 tablespoons olive oil
3 tablespoons dry white wine or water
1½ to 2 pounds mild white fish fillets, such as red snapper
   or sole

Combine salad dressing & seasoning mix, lemon juice, olive oil and wine in a shallow dish; mix well. Add fish and coat all sides with mixture. Cover and refrigerate for 15 to 30 minutes. Remove fish from marinade and place on broiler pan. Broil 9 to 12 minutes or until fish begins to flake when tested with a fork.   *Makes 4 servings*

Hidden Valley® Broiled Fish

Salmon Tortellini

1 package (9 ounces) DI GIORNO® Three Cheese Tortellini, cooked, drained
1 tub (8 ounces) PHILADELPHIA® Cream Cheese with Smoked Salmon
½ cup finely chopped seeded peeled cucumber
1 teaspoon dill weed

PLACE hot tortellini in large bowl.

ADD remaining ingredients; toss lightly. Serve immediately.

Makes 6 to 8 servings

Prep Time: 30 minutes

quick tip

> *For a great substitute, use 2 teaspoons chopped fresh dill in place of dill weed.*

Pan Seared Halibut Steaks with Avocado Salsa

4 tablespoons chipotle salsa, divided
½ teaspoon salt, divided
4 small (4 to 5 ounces) *or* 2 large (8 to 10 ounces) halibut steaks, cut ¾ inch thick
½ cup diced tomato
½ ripe avocado, diced
2 tablespoons chopped cilantro (optional)
Lime wedges (optional)

1. Combine 2 tablespoons salsa and ¼ teaspoon salt; spread over both sides of halibut.

2. Heat large nonstick skillet over medium heat until hot. Add halibut; cook 4 to 5 minutes per side or until fish is opaque in center.

3. Meanwhile, combine remaining 2 tablespoons salsa, ¼ teaspoon salt, tomato, avocado and cilantro, if desired, in small bowl. Mix well and spoon over cooked fish. Garnish with lime wedges, if desired.

Makes 4 servings

Poached Seafood Italiano

1 tablespoon olive or vegetable oil
1 large clove garlic, minced
¼ cup dry white wine or chicken broth
4 (6-ounce) salmon steaks or fillets
1 can (14.5 ounces) CONTADINA® Recipe Ready Diced Tomatoes
    with Italian Herbs, undrained
2 tablespoons chopped fresh basil (optional)

1. Heat oil in large skillet. Add garlic; sauté 30 seconds. Add wine. Bring to boil.

2. Add salmon; cover. Reduce heat to medium; simmer 6 minutes.

3. Add undrained tomatoes; simmer 2 minutes or until salmon flakes easily when tested with fork. Sprinkle with basil just before serving, if desired. *Makes 4 servings*

Poached Seafood Italiano

Lobster Tails with Tasty Butters

Scallion Butter or Chili-Mustard Butter (recipes follow)
4 fresh or thawed frozen lobster tails (about 5 ounces each)

Prepare grill for direct cooking. Prepare 1 butter mixture.

Rinse lobster tails in cold water. Butterfly tails by cutting lengthwise through centers of hard top shells and meat. Cut to, but not through, bottoms of shells. Press shell halves of tails apart with fingers. Brush lobster meat with butter mixture.

Place tails on grid, meat side down. Grill over medium-high heat 4 minutes. Turn tails meat side up. Brush with butter mixture and grill 4 to 5 minutes or until lobster meat turns opaque.

Heat remaining butter mixture, stirring occasionally. Serve butter sauce for dipping. *Makes 4 servings*

Tasty Butters

SCALLION BUTTER
   ⅓ cup butter or margarine, melted
   1 tablespoon finely chopped green onion tops
   1 tablespoon lemon juice
   1 teaspoon grated lemon peel
   ¼ teaspoon black pepper

CHILI-MUSTARD BUTTER
   ⅓ cup butter or margarine, melted
   1 tablespoon chopped onion
   1 tablespoon Dijon mustard
   1 teaspoon chili powder

For each butter sauce, combine ingredients in small bowl.

Lobster Tail with Chili-Mustard Butter

Nutty Pan-Fried Trout

2 tablespoons oil
4 trout fillets (about 6 ounces each)
½ cup seasoned bread crumbs
½ cup pine nuts

1. Heat oil in large skillet over medium heat. Lightly coat fish with crumbs. Add to skillet.

2. Cook 8 minutes or until fish flakes easily when tested with fork, turning after 5 minutes. Remove fish from skillet. Place on serving platter; keep warm.

3. Add nuts to drippings in skillet. Cook and stir 3 minutes or until nuts are lightly toasted. Sprinkle over fish. *Makes 4 servings*

quick tip

Trout fillets can be sprinkled with other toasted nuts, such as almonds, pecans or walnuts.

Creamy Garlic Clam Sauce with Linguine

1 jar (16 ounces) RAGÚ® Cheese Creations!® Roasted Garlic Parmesan Sauce
2 cans (6½ ounces each) chopped clams, undrained
1 tablespoon chopped fresh parsley *or* ½ teaspoon dried parsley flakes
8 ounces linguine or spaghetti, cooked and drained

1. In 3-quart saucepan, cook Ragú Cheese Creations! Sauce, clams and parsley over medium heat, stirring occasionally, 10 minutes.

2. Serve over hot linguine and garnish, if desired, with fresh lemon wedges. *Makes 4 servings*

Prep Time: 5 minutes
Cook Time: 15 minutes

Salmon on a Bed of Leeks

3 to 4 leeks
2 teaspoons butter or margarine
½ cup dry white wine or vermouth
2 salmon fillets (6 to 8 ounces)
**   Salt and black pepper to taste**
2 tablespoons grated Gruyère cheese

Trim green tops and root ends from leeks; cut lengthwise into quarters, leaving ⅓ inch together at root end. Separate sections. Rinse under cold running water; drain well.

In 10-inch skillet, melt butter over medium heat. Add leeks; cook 2 to 3 minutes, stirring often, until leeks are wilted. Stir in wine; arrange salmon on leeks. Sprinkle with salt and pepper. Reduce heat to low. Cover; cook 5 minutes. Sprinkle cheese over salmon. Cover; cook another 3 to 5 minutes or until salmon is firm and opaque around edges and cheese is melted. Transfer to warm dinner plate with broad spatula; serve immediately.   *Makes 2 servings*

*Favorite recipe from **National Fisheries Institute***

Salmon on a Bed of Leeks

Summer Vegetable & Fish Bundles

4 fish fillets (about 1 pound)
1 pound thinly sliced vegetables*
1 envelope LIPTON® RECIPE SECRETS® Savory Herb with Garlic or
**   Golden Onion Soup Mix**
½ cup water

Use any combination of the following: thinly sliced mushrooms, zucchini, yellow squash or tomatoes.

On two 18×18-inch pieces heavy-duty aluminum foil, divide fish equally; top with vegetables. Evenly pour savory herb with garlic soup mix blended with water over fish. Wrap foil loosely around fillets and vegetables, sealing edges airtight with double fold. Grill or broil seam side up 15 minutes or until fish flakes.   *Makes about 4 servings*

quick tip

> Serve this dish over hot cooked rice with Lipton® Iced Tea mixed with a splash of cranberry juice cocktail.

Velveeta® Tuna & Noodles

2¼ cups water
  3 cups (6 ounces) medium egg noodles, uncooked
  ¾ pound (12 ounces) VELVEETA® Pasteurized Prepared Cheese
      Product, cut up
  1 package (16 ounces) frozen vegetable blend, thawed, drained
  1 can (6 ounces) tuna, drained, flaked
  ¼ teaspoon black pepper

1. Bring water to boil in saucepan. Stir in noodles. Reduce heat to medium-low; cover. Simmer 8 minutes or until noodles are tender.

2. Add Velveeta, vegetables, tuna and pepper; stir until Velveeta is melted.   *Makes 4 to 6 servings*

Take a Shortcut: When cooking pasta for Tuna & Noodles, you can double the amount you make and save half for a meal later in the week. Thoroughly drain the pasta you're not using, then put it in a bowl of ice water to stop the cooking. Drain thoroughly, then toss with 1 to 2 teaspoons of oil. Store in a zipper-style plastic bag in the refrigerator for up to 3 days.

Prep Time: 10 minutes
Cook Time: 15 minutes

Scallops with Tomatoes and Basil

8 to 12 large sea scallops, halved crosswise
Salt and freshly ground black pepper, to taste
3 tablespoons FLEISCHMANN'S® Original Margarine, divided
2 tomatoes, peeled, seeded and chopped
2 tablespoons chopped fresh *or* 2 teaspoons dried basil leaves

1. Dry scallops with paper towels; season with salt and pepper.

2. Heat 2 tablespoons margarine in large nonstick skillet over medium-high heat.

3. Arrange half the scallops in a single layer in skillet; cook for 1 to 2 minutes on each side or just until cooked. Transfer scallops to a platter; keep warm. Repeat with remaining scallops; remove to serving platter.

4. Melt remaining margarine in same skillet over medium-high heat. Add tomatoes and basil; heat through.

5. Spoon tomato mixture over the scallops; serve immediately.

Makes 2 servings

Prep Time: 10 minutes
Cook Time: 5 minutes
Total Time: 15 minutes

Scallops with Tomatoes and Basil

Fried Orange Shrimp

 1 cup all-purpose flour
 1 cup Florida orange juice
 1 Florida egg, beaten
 ½ teaspoon salt
    Oil for deep frying
 1½ pounds raw Florida shrimp, peeled and deveined

Combine flour, orange juice, egg and salt; mix well. Heat oil in large skillet to 350°F. Dip shrimp into batter to coat, then place in oil to fry. Cook shrimp about 1 minute or until golden brown. Remove from oil and drain on paper towels. *Makes 6 servings*

Favorite recipe from **Florida Department of Agriculture and Consumer Services, Bureau of Seafood and Aquaculture**

quick tip

> If possible, use a deep-fat thermometer when deep frying. If one is not available, drop a cube of white bread in the hot oil. The bread will brown evenly in 1 minute at approximately 360° to 365°F, 40 seconds at 365° to 370°F, and 20 seconds at 370° to 375°F.

Dilled Salmon in Parchment

2 skinless salmon fillets (4 to 6 ounces each)
2 tablespoons butter or margarine, melted
1 tablespoon lemon juice
1 tablespoon chopped fresh dill
1 tablespoon chopped shallots

1. Preheat oven to 400°F. Cut 2 pieces parchment paper into 12-inch squares; fold squares in half diagonally and cut into half heart shapes. Open parchment; place fish fillet on one side of each heart.

2. Combine butter and lemon juice in small cup; drizzle over fish. Sprinkle with dill, shallots and salt and pepper to taste.

3. Fold parchment hearts in half. Beginning at top of heart, fold edges together, 2 inches at a time. At tip of heart, fold parchment over to seal.

4. Bake fish about 10 minutes or until parchment pouch puffs up. To serve, cut an "X" through top layer of parchment and fold back points to display contents. *Makes 2 servings*

Prep and Cook Time: 20 minutes

Sweet & Zesty Fish with Fruit Salsa

¼ cup *French's*® Zesty Deli Mustard
¼ cup honey
2 cups chopped assorted fresh fruit (pineapple, kiwi, strawberries and mango)
1 pound sea bass or cod fillets or other firm-fleshed white fish

1. Preheat broiler or grill. Combine mustard and honey. Stir *2 tablespoons* mustard mixture into fruit; set aside.

2. Brush remaining mustard mixture on both sides of fillets. Place in foil-lined broiler pan. Broil (or grill) fish 6 inches from heat for 8 minutes or until fish is opaque.

3. Serve fruit salsa with fish. *Makes 4 servings*

Tip: To prepare this meal even faster, purchase cut-up fresh fruit from the salad bar.

Prep Time: 15 minutes
Cook Time: 8 minutes

Sweet & Zesty Fish with Fruit Salsa

Playful
KID FOOD

Ragú® Pizza Burgers

1 pound ground beef
2 cups RAGÚ® Old World Style® Pasta Sauce
1 cup shredded mozzarella cheese (about 4 ounces)
¼ teaspoon salt
6 English muffins, split and toasted

1. In small bowl, combine ground beef, ½ cup Ragú Pasta Sauce, ½ cup cheese and salt. Shape into 6 patties. Grill or broil until done.

2. Meanwhile, heat remaining pasta sauce. To serve, arrange burgers on muffin halves. Top with remaining cheese, sauce and muffin halves.   *Makes 6 servings*

Prep Time: 10 minutes
Cook Time: 15 minutes

Ragú® Pizza Burgers

Fruit Freezies

1½ cups (12 ounces) canned or thawed frozen peach slices, drained
¾ cup peach nectar
1 tablespoon sugar
¼ to ½ teaspoon coconut extract (optional)

1. Place peaches, nectar, sugar and extract in food processor or blender container; process until smooth.

2. Spoon 2 tablespoons fruit mixture into each section of ice cube trays.*

3. Freeze until almost firm. Insert frill pick into each cube; freeze until firm. *Makes 12 servings*

Or, pour ⅓ cup fruit mixture into each of 8 plastic pop molds or small paper or plastic cups. Freeze until almost firm. Insert wooden stick into each mold; freeze until firm. Makes 8 servings.

Apricot Freezies: Substitute canned apricot halves for peach slices and apricot nectar for peach nectar.

Pear Freezies: Substitute canned pear slices for peach slices, pear nectar for peach nectar and almond extract for coconut extract.

Pineapple Freezies: Substitute crushed pineapple for peach slices and unsweetened pineapple juice for peach nectar.

Mango Freezies: Substitute chopped fresh mango for canned peach slices and mango nectar for peach nectar. Omit coconut extract.

Fruit Freezies

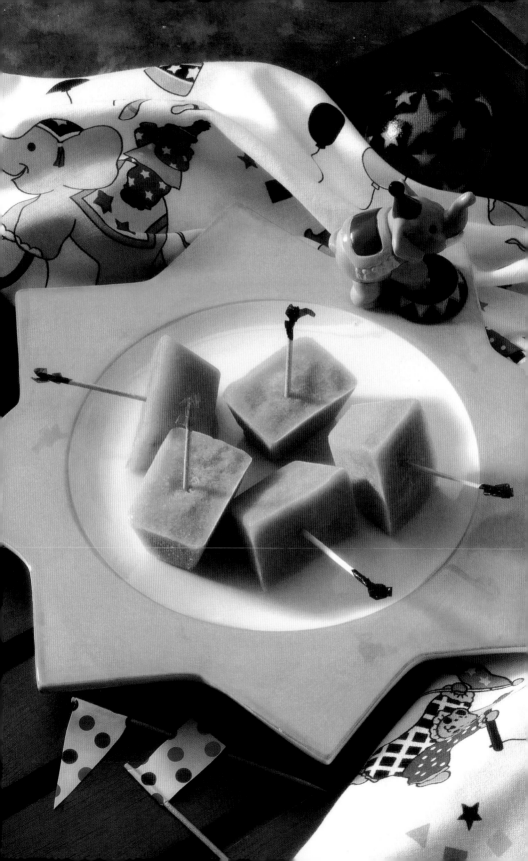

Potato Bugs

1 package (16 ounces) shredded potato nuggets
6 pieces uncooked spaghetti, broken into thirds
1 carrot, cut into 1½-inch strips
   Sour cream, black olive slices, ketchup and broccoli pieces

• Preheat oven to 450°F. Lightly grease baking sheets.

• Spread potato nuggets on baking sheets. Bake 7 minutes. Loosen nuggets from baking sheets with metal spatula.

• Thread 3 potato nuggets onto 1 spaghetti piece. Bake 5 minutes.

• Carefully push carrot strips into sides of each nugget for legs. Using sour cream to attach vegetables, decorate faces of bugs as desired.

Makes about 15 servings

quick tip

For fun bug faces, use black olive slices for eyes and broccoli pieces for antennas. Use ketchup to decorate as desired.

Double-Sauced Chicken Pizza Bagels

1 (about 3½ ounces) whole bagel, split in half
4 tablespoons prepared pizza sauce
½ cup diced cooked chicken breast
¼ cup (1 ounce) shredded part-skim mozzarella cheese
2 teaspoons grated Parmesan cheese

1. Place bagel halves on microwavable plate.

2. Spoon 1 tablespoon pizza sauce onto each bagel half. Spread evenly using back of spoon.

3. Top each bagel half with ¼ cup chicken. Spoon 1 tablespoon pizza sauce over chicken on each bagel half.

4. Sprinkle 2 tablespoons mozzarella cheese over top of each bagel half.

5. Cover bagel halves loosely with waxed paper and microwave at HIGH 1 to 1½ minutes or until cheese melts.

6. Carefully remove waxed paper. Sprinkle each bagel half with 1 teaspoon Parmesan cheese. Let stand 1 minute to cool slightly before eating. (Bagels will be very hot.)

Makes 2 servings (1 bagel half each)

Playful Kid Food

Soft Pretzels

1 package (16 ounces) hot roll mix plus ingredients to prepare mix
1 egg white
2 teaspoons water
2 tablespoons *each* assorted coatings: coarse salt, grated Parmesan cheese, sesame seeds, poppy seeds, dried oregano leaves

1. Prepare hot roll mix according to package directions.

2. Preheat oven to 375°F. Spray baking sheets with nonstick cooking spray; set aside.

3. Divide dough equally into 16 pieces; roll each piece with hands to form a rope, 7 to 10 inches long. Place on prepared cookie sheets; form into desired shape (hearts, wreaths, pretzels, snails, loops, etc.).

4. Beat together egg white and water in small bowl until foamy. Brush onto dough shapes; sprinkle each shape with 1½ teaspoons of one of the coatings.

5. Bake until golden brown, about 15 minutes. Serve warm or at room temperature. *Makes 8 servings*

Fruit Twists: Omit coatings. Prepare dough and roll into ropes as directed. Place ropes on lightly floured surface. Roll out, or pat, each rope into rectangle, ¼ inch thick; brush each rectangle with about 1 teaspoon spreadable fruit or preserves. Fold each rectangle lengthwise in half; twist into desired shape. Bake as directed.

Cheese Twists: Omit coatings. Prepare dough and roll into ropes as directed. Place ropes on lightly floured surface. Roll out, or pat, each rope into rectangle, ¼ inch thick. Sprinkle each rectangle with about 1 tablespoon shredded Cheddar or other flavor cheese. Fold each rectangle lengthwise in half; twist into desired shape. Bake as directed.

Soft Pretzels

Velveeta® Salsa Mac 'n' Cheese

1 pound ground beef
1 jar (16 ounces) chunky salsa
1¾ cups water
2 cups (8 ounces) elbow macaroni
**¾ pound (12 ounces) VELVEETA® Pasteurized Prepared Cheese
     Product, cut up**

Brown beef in large skillet; drain. Add salsa and water. Bring to a boil.
Stir in macaroni. Reduce heat to medium-low; cover. Simmer 8 to
10 minutes or until macaroni are tender. Add Velveeta; stir until
melted.   *Makes 4 to 6 servings*

Grizzly Gorp

2 cups TEDDY GRAHAM® Graham Snacks, any flavor
1 cup JET-PUFFED® Miniature Marshmallows
1 cup PLANTERS® Dry Roasted Peanuts
½ cup seedless raisins

Mix graham snacks, marshmallows, peanuts and raisins. Store in
airtight container.   *Makes 4½ cups*

Golden Chicken Nuggets

1 pound boneless skinless chicken, cut into 1½-inch pieces
¼ cup *French's*® Sweet & Tangy Honey Mustard
2 cups *French's*® French Fried Onions, finely crushed

1. Preheat oven to 400°F. Toss chicken with mustard in medium bowl.

2. Place French Fried Onions into resealable plastic food storage bag. Toss chicken in onions, a few pieces at a time, pressing gently to adhere.

3. Place nuggets in shallow baking pan. Bake 15 minutes or until chicken is no longer pink in center. Serve with additional honey mustard.   *Makes 4 servings*

Prep Time: 5 minutes
Cook Time: 15 minutes

Quick Pizza Snacks

3 English muffins, split and toasted
1 can (14½ ounces) Italian-style diced tomatoes, undrained
¾ cup (3 ounces) shredded Italian cheese blend
Bell pepper strips (optional)

Preheat oven to 350°F. Place English muffin halves on ungreased baking sheet. Top each muffin with ¼ cup tomatoes; sprinkle with 2 tablespoons cheese. Bake about 5 minutes or until cheese is melted and lightly browned. Garnish with bell pepper strips, if desired.

Makes 6 servings

quick tip

> For variety, add other toppings, such as bell peppers, onions, mushrooms or pepperoni, to these delicious pizza snacks.

Quick Pizza Snacks

158

Playful Kid Food

Veggie & Chicken Nuggets

1 bag (16 ounces) BIRDS EYE® frozen Farm Fresh Mixtures Broccoli, Cauliflower & Carrots
1 box (5½ ounces) seasoning & coating mix for chicken (2 packets)
¼ to ½ teaspoon garlic powder
1 pound boneless skinless chicken breast halves, cut into 1½- to 2-inch pieces

• Preheat oven to 400°F.

• Rinse vegetables under warm water to thaw; drain.

• In small bowl, mix coating mix with garlic powder; place ½ of mixture in resealable plastic food storage bag. Add vegetables; shake until evenly coated. Place in single layer on ungreased 15×10-inch baking pan.

• Moisten chicken with water. Add remaining coating mixture and chicken to same bag; shake until evenly coated.

• Place chicken on pan with vegetables, using additional baking pan if too crowded.

• Bake 10 to 15 minutes or until chicken is no longer pink in center.

Makes 4 servings

Serving Suggestion: Serve with a green salad tossed with Italian dressing.

Prep Time: 5 minutes
Cook Time: 15 minutes

Peanut Butter-Pineapple Celery Sticks

½ **cup low-fat (1%) cottage cheese**
½ **cup reduced-fat peanut butter**
½ **cup crushed pineapple in juice, drained**
12 (3-inch-long) celery sticks

Combine cottage cheese and peanut butter in food processor. Blend until smooth. Stir in pineapple. Stuff celery sticks with mixture.

Makes 6 servings

Serving Suggestion: Substitute 2 medium apples, sliced, for celery.

Ham & Cheese Shells & Trees

2 tablespoons margarine or butter
1 (6.2-ounce) package PASTA RONI® Shells & White Cheddar
2 cups fresh or frozen chopped broccoli
⅔ **cup milk**
1½ **cups ham or cooked turkey, cut into thin strips (about 6 ounces)**

1. In large saucepan, bring 2 cups water and margarine to a boil.

2. Stir in pasta. Reduce heat to medium. Gently boil, uncovered, 6 minutes, stirring occasionally. Stir in broccoli; return to a boil. Boil 6 to 8 minutes or until most of water is absorbed.

3. Stir in milk, ham and Special Seasonings. Return to a boil; boil 1 to 2 minutes or until pasta is tender. Let stand 5 minutes before serving.

Makes 4 servings

Tip: No leftovers? Ask the deli to slice a ½-inch-thick piece of ham or turkey.

Prep Time: 5 minutes
Cook Time: 20 minutes

Grilled Cheese & Turkey Shapes

8 slices seedless rye or sourdough bread
8 teaspoons *French's*® Mustard, any flavor
8 slices deli roast turkey
4 slices American cheese
2 tablespoons butter or margarine, softened

1. Spread *1 teaspoon* mustard on each slice of bread. Arrange turkey and cheese on half of the bread slices, dividing evenly. Cover with top halves of bread.

2. Cut out sandwich shapes using choice of cookie cutters. Place cookie cutter on top of sandwich; press down firmly. Remove excess trimmings.

3. Spread butter on both sides of sandwich. Heat large nonstick skillet over medium heat. Cook sandwiches 1 minute per side or until bread is golden and cheese melts.   *Makes 4 sandwiches*

Tip: Use 2½-inch star, heart, teddy bear or flower-shaped cookie cutters.

Prep Time: 15 minutes
Cook Time: 2 minutes

Grilled Cheese & Turkey Shapes

Playful Kid Food

Pizza Rollers

1 package (10 ounces) refrigerated pizza dough
½ cup pizza sauce
18 slices turkey pepperoni
6 sticks mozzarella cheese

1. Preheat oven to 425°F. Coat baking sheet with nonstick cooking spray.

2. Roll out pizza dough on baking sheet to form 12×9-inch rectangle. Cut pizza dough into 6 (4½×4-inch) rectangles. Spread about 1 tablespoon sauce over center third of each rectangle. Top with 3 slices pepperoni and stick of mozzarella cheese. Bring ends of dough together over cheese, pinching to seal. Place, seam side down, on prepared baking sheet.

3. Bake in center of oven 10 minutes or until golden brown.

Makes 6 servings

quick tip

Substitute sausage or vegetables of your choice for the turkey pepperoni in this Pizza Rollers recipe.

Pizza Rollers

Playful Kid Food

Velveeta® Ultimate Grilled Cheese

2 slices bread
2 ounces VELVEETA® Pasteurized Prepared Cheese Product, sliced
2 teaspoons soft margarine

1. Top 1 bread slice with Velveeta and second bread slice.

2. Spread outside of sandwich with margarine.

3. Cook in skillet on medium heat until lightly browned on both sides. *Makes 1 sandwich*

Prep Time: 5 minutes
Cook Time: 10 minutes

quick tip

> Double or triple the ingredients in this recipe to make two or three sandwiches.

Velveeta® Ultimate Grilled Cheese

Banana Smoothies & Pops

1 (14-ounce) can EAGLE® BRAND Sweetened Condensed Milk (NOT evaporated milk)
1 (8-ounce) container vanilla yogurt
2 ripe bananas
½ cup orange juice

Process Eagle Brand and remaining ingredients in blender until smooth, stopping to scrape down sides. Serve immediately.

Makes 4 cups

Banana Smoothie Pops: Spoon banana mixture into 8 (5-ounce) paper cups. Freeze 30 minutes. Insert wooden craft sticks into center of each cup; freeze until firm. Makes 8 pops.

Prep Time: 5 minutes

quick tip

> *To make Fruit Smoothies, substitute 1 cup of your favorite fruit and ½ cup any fruit juice for banana and orange juice.*

Banana Smoothie & Pops

Colorific Pizza Cookie

1 package (17½ ounces) sugar cookie mix
⅔ cup mini candy-coated chocolate pieces
⅓ cup powdered sugar
2 to 3 teaspoons milk

Preheat oven to 375°F.

Prepare cookie mix according to package directions. Spread into ungreased 12-inch pizza pan. Sprinkle evenly with chocolate pieces; press gently into dough.

Bake 20 to 24 minutes or until lightly browned. Cool 2 minutes in pan. Transfer to wire rack and cool completely.

Blend powdered sugar and milk until smooth, adding enough milk to reach drizzling consistency. Drizzle icing over cooled pizza cookie with spoon or fork. Cut into wedges. *Makes 12 servings*

Colorific Pizza Cookie

Smushy Cookies

1 package (20 ounces) refrigerated cookie dough, any flavor
All-purpose flour (optional)

FILLINGS
Peanut butter, multi-colored miniature marshmallows, assorted colored sprinkles, chocolate-covered raisins and caramel candy squares

1. Preheat oven to 350°F. Grease cookie sheets.

2. Remove dough from wrapper according to package directions. Cut into 4 equal sections. Reserve 1 section; refrigerate remaining 3 sections.

3. Roll reserved dough to ¼-inch thickness. Sprinkle with flour to minimize sticking, if necessary. Cut out cookies using 2½-inch round cookie cutter. Transfer to prepared cookie sheets. Repeat with remaining dough, working with 1 section at a time.

4. Bake 8 to 11 minutes or until edges are light golden brown. Remove to wire racks; cool completely.

5. To make sandwich, spread about 1½ tablespoons peanut butter on underside of 1 cookie to within ¼ inch of edge. Sprinkle with miniature marshmallows and candy pieces. Top with second cookie, pressing gently. Repeat with remaining cookies and fillings.

6. Just before serving, place sandwiches on paper towels. Microwave at HIGH 15 to 25 seconds or until fillings become soft.

Makes about 8 to 10 sandwich cookies

Tip: Invite the neighbor kids over on a rainy day to make these fun Smushy Cookies. Be sure to have lots of filling choices available so each child can create his or her own unique cookies.

Smushy Cookies

Peanut Butter-Banana Pops

1 package (16.1 ounces) JELL-O® No Bake Peanut Butter Cup Dessert
1⅓ cups cold milk
1 medium banana, chopped

PLACE Topping Pouch in large bowl of boiling water; set aside.

POUR milk into deep, medium bowl. Add Filling Mix and Peanut Butter Packet. Beat with electric mixer on lowest speed 30 seconds. Beat on highest speed 3 minutes. (Do not underbeat.) Gently stir in Crust Mix and banana. Spoon into 12 paper-lined muffin cups.

REMOVE pouch from water. Knead pouch 60 seconds until fluid and no longer lumpy. Squeeze topping equally over mixture in cups, tilting pan slightly to coat tops. Insert pop sticks into cups.

FREEZE 2 hours or overnight until firm. Remove paper liners.

Makes 12 pops

Note: Wooden pop sticks are sold at craft and hobby stores.

Prep Time: 15 minutes
Freeze Time: 2 hours

Peanut Butter-Banana Pops

Quick S'mores

1 whole graham cracker
1 large marshmallow
1 teaspoon hot fudge sauce

1. Break graham cracker in half crosswise. Place one half on small paper plate or microwavable plate; top with marshmallow.

2. Spread remaining ½ of cracker with fudge sauce.

3. Place cracker with marshmallow in microwave. Microwave at HIGH 12 to 14 seconds or until marshmallow puffs up. Immediately place remaining cracker, fudge side down, over marshmallow. Press crackers gently to even out marshmallow layer. Cool completely.

Makes 1 serving

quick tip

S'mores can be made the night before and wrapped in plastic wrap or sealed in a small plastic food storage bag. Store at room temperature until ready to pack in your child's lunch box the next morning.

Cinnamon Apple Chips

2 cups unsweetened apple juice
1 cinnamon stick
2 Washington Red Delicious apples

1. In large skillet or saucepan, combine apple juice and cinnamon stick; bring to a low boil while preparing apples.

2. With paring knife, slice off ½ inch from tops and bottoms of apples and discard (or eat). Stand apples on either cut end; cut crosswise into ⅛-inch-thick slices, rotating apple as necessary to cut even slices.

3. Drop slices into boiling juice; cook 4 to 5 minutes or until slices appear translucent and lightly golden. Meanwhile, preheat oven to 250°F.

4. With slotted spatula, remove apple slices from juice and pat dry. Arrange slices on wire racks, being sure none overlap. Place racks on middle shelf in oven; bake 30 to 40 minutes until slices are lightly browned and almost dry to touch. Let chips cool on racks completely before storing in airtight container. *Makes about 40 chips*

Tip: There is no need to core apples because boiling in juice for several minutes softens core and removes seeds.

*Favorite recipe from **Washington Apple Commission***

Lollipop Clowns

1 package (18 ounces) refrigerated red, green or blue cookie dough*
All-purpose flour (optional)
Assorted colored icings and hard candies

SUPPLIES
18 (4-inch) lollipop sticks

*If colored dough is unavailable, sugar cookie dough can be tinted with paste food coloring.

1. Preheat oven to 350°F.

2. Remove dough from wrapper according to package directions. Divide dough into 2 equal sections. Reserve 1 section; cover and refrigerate remaining section.

3. Roll out reserved dough on lightly floured surface to ⅛-inch thickness. Sprinkle with flour to minimize sticking, if necessary.

4. Cut out cookies using 3½-inch round cookie cutter. Place lollipop sticks on cookies so that tips of sticks are imbedded in cookies. Carefully turn cookies so sticks are in back; place on ungreased cookie sheets.

5. Bake 8 to 10 minutes or until firm but not brown. Cool on cookie sheets 2 minutes. Remove to wire racks; cool completely.

6. Decorate cookies with icings as shown in photo.

Makes about 18 cookies

Tip: These happy clown faces make the perfect topping for a birthday cake. Stick a Lollipop Clown, one for each child, in the cake for a wonderful circus theme party.

Lollipop Clowns

Musical Instrument Cookies

1 package (18 ounces) refrigerated sugar cookie dough
All-purpose flour (optional)
Assorted colored frostings, colored gels, colored sugars, candy and small decors

1. Preheat oven to 350°F. Grease cookie sheets.

2. Remove dough from wrapper according to package directions. Divide dough into 2 equal sections. Reserve 1 section; cover and refrigerate remaining section.

3. Roll reserved dough on lightly floured surface to ¼-inch thickness. Sprinkle with flour to minimize sticking, if necessary. Cut out cookies using about 3½-inch musical note and instrument cookie cutters. Place cookies 2 inches apart on prepared cookie sheets. Repeat with remaining dough.

4. Bake 10 to 12 minutes or until edges are lightly browned. Remove from oven. Cool on cookie sheets 2 minutes. Remove to wire racks; cool completely.

5. Decorate with colored frostings, gels, sugars and assorted decors as shown in photo. *Makes about 2 dozen cookies*

Musical Instrument Cookies

Playful Kid Food

Cool Sandwich Snacks

10 whole graham crackers or chocolate-flavor graham crackers
½ cup chocolate fudge sauce
1 tub (8 ounces) COOL WHIP® Whipped Topping, thawed
    Suggested Garnishes: Multi-colored sprinkles, assorted candies,
        finely crushed cookies, chocolate chunks, chopped nuts or
        toasted BAKER'S ANGEL FLAKE Coconut

SPREAD ½ of the graham crackers lightly with chocolate sauce. Spread whipped topping about ¾ inch thick on remaining ½ of the graham crackers. Press crackers together lightly, making sandwiches. Roll or lightly press edges in suggested garnish.

FREEZE 4 hours or overnight.   *Makes 10 sandwiches*

Make Ahead: This recipe can be made up to 2 weeks ahead. Wrap well with plastic wrap and freeze.

Prep Time: 15 minutes
Freeze Time: 4 hours

Cool Sandwich Snacks

Dashing
DESSERTS

Dessert Grape Clusters

2 pounds seedless red and/or green grapes
1 pound premium white chocolate, coarsely chopped
2 cups finely chopped honey-roasted cashews
Grape leaves for garnish

1. Rinse grapes under cold running water in colander; drain well. Cut grapes into clusters of 3 grapes with kitchen shears. Place clusters in single layer on paper towels. Let stand at room temperature until completely dry.

2. Melt chocolate in top of double boiler over hot, not boiling, water. Uncover; stir until chocolate is melted. Remove from heat.

3. Place cashews in shallow bowl. Working with 1 cluster at a time and while holding by stem, dip grapes into melted chocolate; allow excess to drain back into pan. Roll grapes gently in cashews. Place grapes, stem side up, on waxed paper; repeat with remaining clusters. Refrigerate until firm. Serve within 4 hours. Garnish, if desired.

Makes about 3 dozen clusters (2½ pounds)

Dessert Grape Clusters

Chocolate Macadamia Chippers

1 package (18 ounces) refrigerated chocolate chip cookie dough
3 tablespoons unsweetened cocoa powder
½ cup coarsely chopped macadamia nuts

Preheat oven to 375°F. Remove dough from wrapper according to package directions.

Place dough in medium bowl; stir in cocoa until well blended. (Dough may be kneaded lightly, if desired.) Stir in nuts. Drop by heaping tablespoons 2 inches apart onto ungreased cookie sheets.

Bake 9 to 11 minutes or until almost set. Transfer to wire racks to cool completely. *Makes 2 dozen cookies*

Chocolate Macadamia Chippers

For You

Apple-Gingerbread Mini Cakes

1 large Cortland or Jonathan apple, cored and quartered
1 package (14½ ounces) gingerbread cake and cookie mix
1 cup water
1 egg
  Powdered sugar

MICROWAVE DIRECTIONS
1. Lightly grease 10 (6- to 7-ounce) custard cups; set aside. Grate apple in food processor or with hand-held grater. Combine grated apple, cake mix, water and egg in medium bowl; stir until well blended. Spoon about ⅓ cup mix into each custard cup, filling cups half full.

2. Arrange 5 cups in microwave. Microwave at HIGH 2 minutes. Rotate cups ½ turn. Microwave 1 minute more or until cakes are springy when touched and look slightly moist on top. Cool on wire rack. Repeat with remaining cakes.

3. To unmold cakes, run a small knife around edge of custard cups to loosen cakes while still warm. Invert on cutting board and tap lightly until cake drops out. Place on plates. When cool enough, dust with powdered sugar, if desired. Serve warm or at room temperature.

Makes 10 cakes

Serving Suggestion: Serve with vanilla ice cream, whipped cream or crème anglaise.

Prep and Cook Time: 20 minutes

Coconut Macaroons

**1 (14-ounce) can EAGLE® BRAND Sweetened Condensed Milk
(NOT evaporated milk)**
2 teaspoons vanilla extract
1 to 1½ teaspoons almond extract
2 (7-ounce) packages flaked coconut (5⅓ cups)

1. Preheat oven to 325°F. Line baking sheets with foil; grease and flour foil. Set aside.

2. In large bowl, combine Eagle Brand, vanilla and almond extract. Stir in coconut. Drop by rounded teaspoonfuls onto prepared sheets; with spoon, slightly flatten each mound.

3. Bake 15 to 17 minutes or until golden. Remove from baking sheets; cool on wire racks. Store loosely covered at room temperature.

Makes about 4 dozen cookies

Prep Time: 10 minutes
Bake Time: 15 to 17 minutes

Fudgy Milk Chocolate Fondue

1 (16-ounce) can chocolate-flavored syrup
1 (14-ounce) can EAGLE® BRAND Sweetened Condensed Milk
    (NOT evaporated milk)
  Dash salt
1½ teaspoons vanilla extract
    Assorted dippers: cookies, cake, pound cake cubes, angel food
    cake cubes, banana chunks, apple slices, strawberries, pear
    slices, kiwifruit slices and/or marshmallows

1. In heavy saucepan over medium heat, combine syrup, Eagle Brand and salt. Cook and stir 12 to 15 minutes or until slightly thickened.

2. Remove from heat; stir in vanilla. Serve warm with assorted dippers. Store covered in refrigerator.   *Makes about 3 cups*

Microwave Directions: In 1-quart glass measure, combine syrup, Eagle Brand and salt. Cook at HIGH (100% power) 3½ to 4 minutes, stirring after 2 minutes. Stir in vanilla.

Tip: Can be served warm or cold over ice cream. Can be made several weeks ahead. Store tightly covered in refrigerator.

Prep Time: 12 to 15 minutes

Fudgy Milk Chocolate Fondue

Speedy Pineapple-Lime Sorbet

1 ripe pineapple, cut into cubes (about 4 cups)
⅓ cup frozen limeade concentrate, thawed
1 to 2 tablespoons fresh lime juice
1 teaspoon grated lime peel

1. Arrange pineapple in single layer on large sheet pan; freeze at least 1 hour or until very firm. Use metal spatula to transfer pineapple to resealable plastic freezer food storage bags; freeze up to 1 month.

2. Combine pineapple, limeade, lime juice and lime peel in food processor; process until smooth and fluffy. If pineapple doesn't become smooth and fluffy, let stand 30 minutes to soften slightly; then repeat processing. Serve immediately. Garnish as desired.

Makes 8 (½-cup) servings

quick tip

This sorbet is best if served immediately, but may be made ahead, stored in the freezer and softened several minutes before serving.

Speedy Pineapple-Lime Sorbet

Chocolate Mint Ravioli Cookies

1 package (15 ounces) refrigerated pie crusts
1 bar (7 ounces) cookies 'n' mint chocolate candy
1 egg
1 tablespoon water
  Powdered sugar

1. Preheat oven to 400°F. Unfold 1 pie crust on lightly floured surface. Roll into 13-inch circle. Using 2½-inch cutters, cut pastry into 24 circles, rerolling scraps if necessary. Repeat with remaining pie crust.

2. Separate candy bar into pieces marked on bar. Cut each chocolate piece in half. Beat egg and water together in small bowl with fork. Brush half of pastry circles lightly with egg mixture. Place 1 piece of chocolate in center of each circle (there will be some candy bar left over). Top with remaining pastry circles. Seal edges with tines of fork.

3. Place on *ungreased* baking sheets. Brush with egg mixture.

4. Bake 8 to 10 minutes or until golden brown. Remove from cookie sheets; cool completely on wire racks. Dust with powdered sugar.

Makes 2 dozen cookies

Tip: Mix it up! Substitute your favorite candy bar for the cookies 'n' mint chocolate candy for a completely different taste.

Prep and Cook Time: 30 minutes

Chocolate Mint Ravioli Cookies

Banana Cream Parfaits

1 package (4 serving size) sugar-free vanilla pudding and pie filling mix
2 cups low-fat (1%) milk
1 cup coarsely crushed sugar-free cookies
2 large ripe bananas, peeled and sliced
  Mint sprigs (optional)

1. Prepare pudding according to package directions using low-fat milk; cool 10 minutes, stirring occasionally.

2. In parfait or wine glasses, layer 2 tablespoons cookie crumbs, ¼ cup banana slices and ¼ cup pudding. Repeat layering. Cover; chill at least 1 hour or up to 6 hours before serving. Garnish with mint sprigs, if desired. *Makes 4 servings*

Variation: Sugar-free chocolate pudding and pie filling mix may be substituted for vanilla pudding.

Prep Time: 20 minutes
Cook Time: 5 minutes
Chill Time: at least 1 hour

Dashing Desserts

Toffee Creme Sandwich Cookies

1 jar (7 ounces) marshmallow creme
¼ cup toffee baking pieces
48 (2-inch) sugar or fudge-striped shortbread cookies
Red and green sprinkles

1. Combine marshmallow creme and toffee pieces in medium bowl until well blended. (Mixture will be stiff.)

2. Spread 1 teaspoon marshmallow mixture on bottom of 1 cookie; top with another cookie. Roll side of sandwich cookie in sprinkles. Repeat with remaining marshmallow creme mixture, cookies and sprinkles. *Makes 2 dozen cookies*

Prep Time: 20 minutes

quick tip

Choose different colors of sprinkles to represent your favorite sports team or even just your favorite colors.

Spun Sugar Berries with Yogurt Crème

2 cups fresh raspberries*
**1 container (8 ounces) lemon-flavored nonfat yogurt with
    aspartame sweetener**
1 cup thawed frozen fat-free nondairy whipped topping
3 tablespoons sugar

*You may substitute your favorite fresh berries for the fresh raspberries.

1. Arrange berries in 4 glass dessert dishes.

2. Combine yogurt and whipped topping in medium bowl. (If not using immediately, cover and refrigerate.) Top berries with yogurt mixture.

3. To prepare spun sugar, pour sugar into heavy medium saucepan. Cook over medium-high heat until sugar melts, shaking pan occasionally. *Do not stir.* As sugar begins to melt, reduce heat to low and cook about 10 minutes or until sugar is completely melted and has turned light golden brown.

4. Remove from heat; let stand for 1 minute. Coat metal fork with sugar mixture. Drizzle sugar over berries with circular or back and forth motion. Ropes of spun sugar will harden quickly. Garnish as desired. Serve immediately.   *Makes 4 servings*

Spun Sugar Berries with Yogurt Crème

Triple Layer Chocolate Mints

6 ounces semisweet chocolate, chopped
6 ounces white chocolate, chopped
1 teaspoon peppermint extract
6 ounces milk chocolate, chopped

1. Line 8-inch square pan with foil, leaving 1-inch overhang on sides.

2. Place semisweet chocolate in top of double boiler over simmering water. Stir until melted. Remove from heat.

3. Spread melted chocolate onto bottom of prepared pan. Let stand until firm. (If not firm after 45 minutes, refrigerate 10 minutes.)

4. Melt white chocolate in clean double boiler; stir in peppermint extract. Spread over semisweet chocolate layer. Shake pan to spread evenly. Let stand 45 minutes or until set.

5. Melt milk chocolate in same double boiler. Spread over white chocolate layer. Shake pan to spread evenly. Let stand 45 minutes or until set.

6. Cut mints into 16 (2-inch) squares. Remove from pan by lifting mints and foil with foil handles. Place squares on cutting board.

7. Cut each square diagonally into 2 triangles. Cut in half again to make 64 small triangles. Store in airtight container in refrigerator.

Makes 64 mints

Triple Layer Chocolate Mints

Cheesecake Creme Dip

1 package (8 ounces) PHILADELPHIA® Cream Cheese, softened
1 jar (7 ounces) JET-PUFFED® Marshmallow Creme

BEAT cream cheese and marshmallow creme with electric mixer on medium speed until well blended; cover. Refrigerate several hours or until chilled.

SERVE with assorted cut-up fresh fruit or pound cake cubes. Garnish, if desired.   *Makes 1¾ cups*

Prep Time: 5 minutes plus refrigerating

quick tip

> *Peaches, strawberries, raspberries and orange slices are delicious choices to serve with this dip.*

Cheesecake Creme Dip

Sinfully Simple Chocolate Cake

1 package (18¼ ounces) chocolate cake mix plus ingredients to prepare mix
1 cup whipping cream, chilled
⅓ cup chocolate syrup
Fresh fruit for garnish (optional)

Prepare cake mix according to package directions for two 8- or 9-inch layers. Cool layers completely.

Beat whipping cream with electric mixer at high speed until it begins to thicken. Gradually add chocolate syrup; continue beating until soft peaks form.

To assemble, place one cake layer on serving plate; spread half of whipped cream mixture over top. Set second cake layer on top; spread remaining whipped cream mixture over top. Garnish, if desired. Store in refrigerator.   *Makes 12 servings*

Sinfully Simple Chocolate Cake

Walnut Meringues

3 egg whites
Pinch salt
¾ cup sugar
⅓ cup finely chopped walnuts

Preheat oven to 350°F. Line baking sheet with parchment paper. Place egg whites and salt in large bowl. Beat until soft peaks form. Gradually add sugar, beating until stiff peaks form. Gently fold in walnuts. Drop mounds about 1 inch in diameter 1 inch apart onto prepared baking sheet. Bake 20 minutes or until lightly browned and dry to the touch. Let cool completely before removing from baking sheet. Store in airtight container.   *Makes 48 cookies*

Strawberry-Banana Granité

2 ripe medium bananas, peeled and sliced (about 2 cups)
2 cups unsweetened frozen strawberries *(do not thaw)*
¼ cup no-sugar-added strawberry pourable fruit*
Whole fresh strawberries (optional)
Fresh mint leaves (optional)

*3 tablespoons no-sugar-added strawberry fruit spread combined with 1 tablespoon warm water may be substituted.

Place banana slices in plastic bag; freeze until firm. Place frozen banana slices and frozen strawberries in food processor container. Let stand 10 minutes for fruit to soften slightly. Add pourable fruit. Remove plunger from top of food processor to allow air to be incorporated. Process until smooth, scraping down sides of container frequently. Serve immediately. Garnish with fresh strawberries and mint leaves, if desired. Freeze leftovers.   *Makes 5 servings*

Note: Granité may be transferred to airtight container and frozen up to 1 month. Let stand at room temperature 10 minutes to soften slightly before serving.

Dashing Desserts

Oreo® Brownie Treats

15 OREO® Chocolate Sandwich Cookies, coarsely chopped
1 (21½-ounce) package deluxe fudge brownie mix, batter prepared according to package directions
2 pints ice cream, any flavor

1. Stir cookie pieces into prepared brownie batter. Pour into greased 13×9-inch baking pan.

2. Bake according to brownie mix package directions for time and temperature. Cool.

3. To serve, cut into 12 squares and top each with a scoop of ice cream. *Makes 12 servings*

Thumbprints

1 package (20 ounces) refrigerated sugar or chocolate cookie dough
All-purpose flour (optional)
¾ cup plus 1 tablespoon fruit preserves, any flavor

1. Grease cookie sheets. Remove dough from wrapper according to package directions. Sprinkle with flour to minimize sticking, if necessary.

2. Cut dough into 26 (1-inch) slices. Roll slices into balls, sprinkling with additional flour, if necessary. Place balls 2 inches apart on prepared cookie sheets. Press deep indentation in center of each ball with thumb. Freeze dough 20 minutes.

3. Preheat oven to 350°F. Bake cookies 12 to 13 minutes or until edges are light golden brown (cookies will have started to puff up and lose their shape). Quickly press down indentation using tip of teaspoon.

4. Return to oven 2 to 3 minutes or until cookies are golden brown and set. Cool cookies completely on cookie sheets. Fill each indentation with about 1½ teaspoons preserves.

Makes 26 cookies

Tip: These cookies are just as delicious filled with peanut butter or melted semisweet chocolate chips.

Thumbprints

Chocolate Baskets with Berries

4 to 6 ounces semisweet or bittersweet chocolate, chopped
1 cup fresh blueberries, raspberries or sliced strawberries
2 tablespoons Grand Marnier, Chambord, Cointreau or sugar
1 cup frozen raspberry yogurt or sorbet

1. Invert two 6-ounce custard cups onto baking sheet. Cover each cup with piece of foil, smoothing surface to make sure foil stays in place. Coat cups with nonstick cooking spray.

2. Melt chocolate in small heavy saucepan over low heat. Remove from heat; let stand 10 minutes. Spoon into pastry bag fitted with small writing tip.

3. Slowly drizzle chocolate over each cup. (If chocolate drizzles too fast, let cool. If it becomes too firm, remove from bag and reheat.) Refrigerate 10 minutes. Repeat procedure; refrigerate 1 hour. Carefully remove custard cups and foil from baskets. Store in airtight container in refrigerator until ready to serve.

4. Combine fruit and liqueur in small bowl. Cover and refrigerate until ready to serve.

5. To complete recipe, spoon frozen yogurt into chocolate baskets on serving plates. Spoon fruit mixture evenly over yogurt and around chocolate baskets. Garnish as desired.   *Makes 2 servings*

Make-Ahead Time: up to 1 day before serving
Final Prep and Cook Time: 5 minutes

Chocolate Basket with Berries

Surprise Cookies

1 package (18 ounces) refrigerated sugar cookie dough
All-purpose flour (optional)
Any combination of walnut halves, whole almonds, chocolate-covered raisins or caramel candy squares for filling
Assorted colored sugars

1. Grease cookie sheets. Remove dough from wrapper according to package directions. Divide dough into 4 equal sections. Reserve 1 section; cover and refrigerate remaining 3 sections.

2. Roll reserved dough to ¼-inch thickness. Sprinkle with flour to minimize sticking, if necessary. Cut out 3-inch square cookie with sharp knife. Transfer cookie to prepared cookie sheet.

3. Place desired "surprise" filling in center of cookie. (If using caramel candy square, place so that caramel forms diamond shape within square.)

4. Bring up 4 corners of dough towards center; pinch gently to seal. Repeat steps with remaining dough and fillings, placing cookies about 2 inches apart on prepared cookie sheets. Sprinkle with colored sugar, if desired. Freeze cookies 20 minutes. Preheat oven to 350°F.

5. Bake 9 to 11 minutes or until edges are lightly browned. Remove to wire racks; cool completely.   *Makes about 14 cookies*

Tip: Make extra batches of these simple cookies and store in freezer in heavy-duty freezer bags. Take out a few at a time for kids' after-school treats.

Surprise Cookies

Buttery Peppermints

20 hard peppermint candies, unwrapped
5½ cups powdered sugar, divided
⅓ cup evaporated milk
¼ cup butter

1. Place peppermint candies and ½ cup powdered sugar in food processor; process using on/off pulsing action until consistency of powder.

2. Heat evaporated milk, butter and ½ cup powdered candy mixture in heavy large saucepan over medium-low heat until candy dissolves and mixture just begins to boil, stirring constantly. Transfer to large bowl. Set aside remaining powdered candy mixture.

3. Stir 4 cups powdered sugar into milk mixture with wooden spoon until well blended. Stir in additional powdered sugar, ¼ cup at a time, until consistency of dough. Place on surface lightly dusted with powdered sugar.

4. Knead dough until smooth. Divide dough into 4 equal portions.

5. Roll each portion into 20-inch-long roll. Cut each roll into ¾-inch pieces. Roll in reserved powdered candy mixture to coat.

6. For soft mints, store in airtight container at room temperature. For dry mints, keep uncovered several hours before storing in airtight container. *Makes about 8 dozen mints*

Strawberry Shortcut

1 package (10 to 12 ounces) frozen pound cake, cut into 14 slices
3 cups strawberries, sliced, sweetened
1 tub (8 ounces) COOL WHIP® Whipped Topping, thawed

PLACE 7 of the cake slices on individual dessert plates.

SPOON about 3 tablespoons of the strawberries over each cake slice. Top each with ¼ cup whipped topping. Repeat layers, ending with a dollop of whipped topping. Garnish as desired. Serve immediately.

Makes 7 servings

Prep Time: 10 minutes

Choco-Peanut Pinwheels

1 cup (6 ounces) peanut butter-flavored chips
1 (14-ounce) can EAGLE® BRAND Sweetened Condensed Milk
   (NOT evaporated milk), divided
1 cup (6 ounces) semi-sweet chocolate chips
1 teaspoon vanilla extract

1. Cut waxed paper into 15×10-inch rectangle; butter paper.

2. In heavy saucepan, over low heat, melt peanut butter chips with ⅔ cup Eagle Brand. Cool slightly. With fingers, press evenly into thin layer to cover waxed paper. Let stand at room temperature 15 minutes.

3. In heavy saucepan, melt chocolate chips with remaining Eagle Brand. Remove from heat; stir in vanilla. Spread evenly over peanut butter layer. Let stand at room temperature 30 minutes.

4. Beginning at 15-inch side, roll up tightly, jelly-roll fashion, without waxed paper. Wrap tightly in plastic wrap.

5. Chill 2 hours or until firm. Cut into ¼-inch slices to serve. Store covered at room temperature.

Makes about 1½ pounds

Prep Time: 15 minutes
Chill Time: 2 hours

Luscious Chocolate Covered Strawberries

3 squares (1 ounce each) semi-sweet chocolate
2 tablespoons I CAN'T BELIEVE IT'S NOT BUTTER!® Spread
1 tablespoon coffee liqueur (optional)
6 to 8 large strawberries with stems

In small microwave-safe bowl, microwave chocolate and I Can't Believe It's Not Butter! Spread at HIGH (Full Power) 1 minute or until chocolate is melted; stir until smooth. Stir in liqueur, if desired. Dip strawberries in chocolate mixture, then refrigerate on waxed paper-lined baking sheet until chocolate is set, at least 1 hour.

Makes 6 to 8 strawberries

Luscious Chocolate Covered Strawberries

The publisher would like to thank the companies and organizations listed below for the use of their recipes and photographs in this publication.

A.1.® Steak Sauce
BelGioioso® Cheese, Inc.
Birds Eye®
Butterball® Turkey Company
Del Monte Corporation
Eagle® Brand
Fleischmann's® Original Spread
Florida Department of Agriculture and Consumer Services,
Bureau of Seafood and Aquaculture
The Golden Grain Company®
The Hidden Valley® Food Products Company
Hormel Foods, LLC
Holland House® is a registered trademark of Mott's, Inc.
Kraft Foods Holdings
Lawry's® Foods, Inc.
Lee Kum Kee (USA) Inc.
Nabisco Biscuit and Snack Division
National Fisheries Institute
National Pork Board
OREO® Chocolate Sandwich Cookies
Perdue Farms Incorporated
Reckitt Benckiser
Riviana Foods Inc.
The J.M. Smucker Company
Tyson Foods, Inc.
Unilever Bestfoods North America
USA Rice Federation

218

A
Apple Blossom Mold, 52
Apple-Gingerbread Mini Cakes, 188
Apples
  Apple Blossom Mold, 52
  Apple-Gingerbread Mini Cakes,
    188
  Cinnamon Apple Chips, 177
  Hickory Pork Tenderloin with
    Apple Topping, 110
Apricot
  Apricot Freezies, 150
  Baked Apricot Brie, 22
  Sunshine Chicken Drumsticks, 8
Arizona Cheese Crisp, 10
Asian Chicken and Noodles, 61

B
Bacon
  Bacon-Wrapped Breadsticks, 6
  Cheddar Tomato Bacon Toasts, 16
Baked Apricot Brie, 22
Bananas
  Banana Cream Parfaits, 196
  Banana Smoothie Pops, 168
  Banana Smoothies & Pops, 168
  Peanut Butter-Banana Pops, 174
  Strawberry-Banana Granité, 206
Barbecue Pork Skillet, 120
Beef, Ground
  Beefy Mac & Double Cheddar, 92
  Blue Cheese Burgers, 106
  Cheeseburger Soup, 93
  Cheesy Spinach Burgers, 90
  Ragú® Pizza Burgers, 148
  Skillet Pasta Dinner, 104
  Souper Stuffed Cheese Burgers,
    87
  Ultimate The Original Ranch®
    Cheese Burgers, 100
  Velveeta® Beef Enchiladas Olé, 88
  Velveeta® Salsa Mac, 98
  Velveeta® Salsa Mac 'n' Cheese,
    156
Beefy Mac & Double Cheddar, 92
BelGioioso® Fontina Melt, 25
Blue Cheese Burgers, 106
Blueberries: Chocolate Baskets with
    Berries, 210

Breads
  Bacon-Wrapped Breadsticks, 6
  Cheese Twists, 154
  Fast Pesto Focaccia, 28
  French Onion Bread Stix, 33
  Fruit Twists, 154
  Garlic Bread, 41
  Soft Pretzels, 154
  Zesty Bruschetta, 13
Broccoli
  Broccoli-Cheese Quesadillas, 13
  Ham & Cheese Shells & Trees, 161
  1-2-3 Cheddar Broccoli Casserole,
    34
  Velveeta® 15 Minute Cheesy Rice
    with Ham & Broccoli, 112
Brown Rice Royal, 36
Buffalo-Style Shrimp, 8
Butterflied Cornish Game Hens, 82
Buttery Peppermints, 214

C
Cajun Chicken Bayou, 68
Cakes
  Apple-Gingerbread Mini Cakes,
    188
  Sinfully Simple Chocolate Cake,
    204
  Strawberry Shortcut, 215
Can't Get Enough Chicken Wings, 12
Caribbean Jerk Chicken with Quick
    Fruit Salsa, 61
Carrots
  Herbed Chicken & Vegetables, 69
  Honey-Glazed Carrots and
    Parsnips, 46
Casseroles
  Creamed Spinach Casserole, 36
  One-Dish Meal, 76
  1-2-3 Cheddar Broccoli Casserole,
    34
Cheddar Tomato Bacon Toasts, 16
Cheeseburger Soup, 93
Cheesecake Creme Dip, 202
Cheese Twists, 154
Cheesy Spinach Burgers, 90
Chili Garlic Prawns, 18
Chili-Mustard Butter, 134
Choco-Peanut Pinwheels, 215

Chocolate
  Chocolate Baskets with Berries, 210
  Chocolate Macadamia Chippers, 186
  Chocolate Mint Ravioli Cookies, 194
  Choco-Peanut Pinwheels, 215
  Colorific Pizza Cookie, 170
  Cool Sandwich Snacks, 182
  Fudgy Milk Chocolate Fondue, 190
  Luscious Chocolate Covered Strawberries, 216
  Oreo® Brownie Treats, 207
  Peanut Butter-Banana Pops, 174
  Quick S'mores, 176
  Sinfully Simple Chocolate Cake, 204
  Triple Layer Chocolate Mints, 200
Chocolate Baskets with Berries, 210
Chocolate Macadamia Chippers, 186
Chocolate Mint Ravioli Cookies, 194
Chorizo Cheese Crisp, 10
Cinnamon Apple Chips, 177
Classic Fried Chicken, 58
Classic Polenta, 38
Coconut Macaroons, 189
Colorific Pizza Cookie, 170
Cookies
  Chocolate Macadamia Chippers, 186
  Chocolate Mint Ravioli Cookies, 194
  Choco-Peanut Pinwheels, 215
  Coconut Macaroons, 189
  Colorific Pizza Cookie, 170
  Lollipop Clowns, 178
  Musical Instrument Cookies, 180
  Smushy Cookies, 172
  Surprise Cookies, 212
  Thumbprints, 208
  Toffee Creme Sandwich Cookies, 197
  Walnut Meringues, 206
Cool Sandwich Snacks, 182

Corn
  Grilled Turkey with Roasted Garlic Grilled Corn, 80
  Herbed Corn on the Cob, 30
Cottage Fried Potatoes, 32
Country Herb Roasted Chicken, 60
Creamed Spinach Casserole, 36
Creamy Garlic Clam Sauce with Linguine, 137
Crispy Ranch Chicken, 74
Crostini, 25
Cucumber
  Peas with Cukes 'n' Dill, 46
  Salmon Tortellini, 130
Cure 81® Ham with Honey Mustard Glaze, 120
Cutlets Milanese, 79

D
Dessert Grape Clusters, 184
Di Giorno® Easy Chicken Cacciatore with Light Ravioli, 70
Dilled Salmon in Parchment, 145
Double-Sauced Chicken Pizza Bagels, 153

F
Fast Pesto Focaccia, 28
Fish & Shellfish (see pages 128–147)
  Buffalo-Style Shrimp, 8
  Chili Garlic Prawns, 18
Fragrant Beef with Garlic Sauce, 94
French Onion Bread Stix, 33
Fresh Vegetable Sauté, 42
Fried Orange Shrimp, 144
Fruit Freezies, 150
Fruit Twists, 154
Fudgy Milk Chocolate Fondue, 190

G
Garlic Bread, 41
Garlic Mushroom Chicken Melt, 54
Garlic Pork Chops, 121
Golden Chicken Nuggets, 157
Grilled Cheese & Turkey Shapes, 162
Grilled Rosemary Chicken, 62
Grilled Sauerbraten Steak, 105
Grilled Sherry Pork Chops, 108

Index

Grilled Turkey with Roasted Garlic
    Grilled Corn, 80
Grizzly Gorp, 156

H
Ham
    Cure 81® Ham with Honey
        Mustard Glaze, 120
    Ham & Cheese Shells & Trees, 161
    Orange Mustard Ham Kabobs,
        122
    Velveeta® 15 Minute Cheesy Rice
        with Ham & Broccoli, 112
Ham & Cheese Shells & Trees, 161
Herbed Chicken & Vegetables, 69
Herbed Corn on the Cob, 30
Herbed Green Beans, 40
Hickory Pork Tenderloin with Apple
    Topping, 110
Hidden Valley Ranch® Cheese
    Fingers, 18
Hidden Valley® Broiled Fish, 128
Honey-Glazed Carrots and Parsnips,
    46
Hot & Spicy Buffalo Chicken Wings,
    24

L
Lean Homemade Sausage, 113
Lemon: Lemon-Capered Pork
    Tenderloin, 118
Lobster Tails with Tasty Butters, 134
Lollipop Clowns, 178
Luscious Chocolate Covered
    Strawberries, 216

M
Marinated Flank Steak with
    Pineapple, 96
Marinated Pork Roast, 126
Marshmallows
    Grizzly Gorp, 156
    Quick S'mores, 176
Mexican Roll-Ups, 14
Mixed Vegetables
    Asian Chicken and Noodles, 61
    Oven-Roasted Vegetables, 48
    Vegetable-Stuffed Baked
        Potatoes, 42

Mixed Vegetables *(continued)*
    Veggie & Chicken Nuggets, 160
    Velveeta® Tuna & Noodles, 141
Mushrooms
    Brown Rice Royal, 36
    Garlic Mushroom Chicken Melt, 54
Musical Instrument Cookies, 180

N
Nuts
    Chocolate Macadamia Chippers,
        186
    Dessert Grape Clusters, 184
    Grizzly Gorp, 156
    Nutty Pan-Fried Trout, 136
    Summer Raspberry Chicken, 56
    Walnut Meringues, 206
Nutty Pan-Fried Trout, 136

O
Olive Cheese Crisp, 10
One-Dish Meal, 76
1-2-3 Cheddar Broccoli Casserole, 34
Onion-Baked Pork Chops, 116
Onion-Roasted Potatoes, 30
Orange
    Banana Smoothie Pops, 168
    Banana Smoothies & Pops, 168
    Fried Orange Shrimp, 144
    Orange Mustard Ham Kabobs, 122
Oreo® Brownie Treats, 207
Oven-Roasted Vegetables, 48

P
Pan Seared Halibut Steaks with
    Avocado Salsa, 131
Pasta
    Asian Chicken and Noodles, 61
    Beefy Mac & Double Cheddar, 92
    Creamy Garlic Clam Sauce with
        Linguine, 137
    Di Giorno® Easy Chicken
        Cacciatore with Light Ravioli, 70
    Ham & Cheese Shells & Trees,
        161
    Mexican Roll-Ups, 14
    Salmon Tortellini, 130
    Skillet Pasta Dinner, 104
    Velveeta® Salsa Mac, 98

Pasta *(continued)*
  Velveeta® Salsa Mac 'n' Cheese, 156
  Velveeta® Tuna & Noodles, 141
  Velveeta® Ultimate Macaroni & Cheese, 44
Peanut Butter
  Peanut Butter-Banana Pops, 174
  Peanut Butter-Pineapple Celery Sticks, 161
Pear Freezies, 150
Peas
  One-Dish Meal, 76
  Peas with Cukes 'n' Dill, 46
Peppered Pork Tenderloin, 114
Peppers, Bell
  Di Giorno® Easy Chicken Cacciatore with Light Ravioli, 70
  Roasted Sweet Pepper Tapas, 19
  Peppery Turkey Fillets, 78
Pineapple
  Marinated Flank Steak with Pineapple, 96
  Peanut Butter-Pineapple Celery Sticks, 161
  Pineapple Freezies, 150
  Speedy Pineapple-Lime Sorbet, 192
Pineapple Freezies, 150
Pizza Rollers, 164
Poached Seafood Italiano, 132
Pork Chops with Balsamic Vinegar, 124
Potato Bugs, 152
Potatoes
  Cottage Fried Potatoes, 32
  Herbed Chicken & Vegetables, 69
  Onion-Roasted Potatoes, 30
  Potato Bugs, 152
  Roasted Idaho & Sweet Potatoes, 50
  Swiss Rosti Potatoes, 47
  Vegetable-Stuffed Baked Potatoes, 42
Poultry *(see pages 54–83)*
  Can't Get Enough Chicken Wings, 12
  Double-Sauced Chicken Pizza Bagels, 153

Poultry *(continued)*
  Golden Chicken Nuggets, 157
  Grilled Cheese & Turkey Shapes, 162
  Hot & Spicy Buffalo Chicken Wings, 24
  Sunshine Chicken Drumsticks, 8
  Veggie & Chicken Nuggets, 160
Prime Rib, 86

Q
Quick Pizza Snacks, 158
Quick S'mores, 176

R
Ragú® Pizza Burgers, 148
Raspberry
  Chocolate Baskets with Berries, 210
  Spun Sugar Berries with Yogurt Crème, 198
  Summer Raspberry Chicken, 56
Rice
  Brown Rice Royal, 36
  Cajun Chicken Bayou, 68
  One-Dish Meal, 76
  Velveeta® Cheesy Chicken & Rice Skillet, 66
  Velveeta® 15 Minute Cheesy Rice with Ham & Broccoli, 112
Roasted Chicken au Jus, 72
Roasted Idaho & Sweet Potatoes, 50
Roasted Sweet Pepper Tapas, 19
Roast Stuffed Turkey, 79

S
Salmon on a Bed of Leeks, 138
Salmon Tortellini, 130
Sandwiches & Burgers
  Blue Cheese Burgers, 106
  Cheesy Spinach Burgers, 90
  Grilled Cheese & Turkey Shapes, 162
  Ragú® Pizza Burgers, 148
  Souper Stuffed Cheese Burgers, 87
  Ultimate The Original Ranch® Cheese Burgers, 100
  Velveeta® Ultimate Grilled Cheese, 166

Index

Sausage
  Chorizo Cheese Crisp, 10
  Lean Homemade Sausage, 113
Scallion Butter, 134
Scallops with Tomatoes and Basil, 142
Sinfully Simple Chocolate Cake, 204
Skillet Pasta Dinner, 104
Smushy Cookies, 172
Soft Pretzels, 154
Souper Stuffed Cheese Burgers, 87
Speedy Pineapple-Lime Sorbet, 192
Spicy Fried Chicken, 58
Spinach
  Cheesy Spinach Burgers, 90
  Creamed Spinach Casserole, 36
  Spinach Cheese Bundles, 20
  Stir-Fried Beef & Spinach, 101
Spun Sugar Berries with Yogurt
  Crème, 198
Steakhouse London Broil, 102
Stir-Fried Beef & Spinach, 101
Strawberries
  Luscious Chocolate Covered
    Strawberries, 216
  Strawberry Shortcut, 215
  Strawberry-Banana Granité, 206
Summer Raspberry Chicken, 56
Summer Vegetable & Fish Bundles,
  140
Sunshine Chicken Drumsticks, 8
Super Nachos, 26
Surprise Cookies, 212
Sweet & Zesty Fish with Fruit Salsa,
  146
Swiss Rosti Potatoes, 47

T
Tender Baked Chicken, 70
Thumbprints, 208
Toffee Creme Sandwich Cookies, 197
Tomatoes, Canned
  Cajun Chicken Bayou, 68
  Garlic Mushroom Chicken Melt, 54
  Poached Seafood Italiano, 132
  Quick Pizza Snacks, 158
Tomatoes, Fresh
  BelGioioso® Fontina Melt, 25
  Cheddar Tomato Bacon Toasts, 16
  Cheeseburger Soup, 93

Tomatoes, Fresh (continued)
  Crostini, 25
  Pan Seared Halibut Steaks with
    Avocado Salsa, 131
  Scallops with Tomatoes and Basil,
    142
Tortillas
  Arizona Cheese Crisp, 10
  Broccoli-Cheese Quesadillas, 13
  Chorizo Cheese Crisp, 10
  Olive Cheese Crisp, 10
  Velveeta® Beef Enchiladas Olé, 88
Triple Layer Chocolate Mints, 200

U
Ultimate The Original Ranch®
  Cheese Burgers, 100

V
Vegetable-Stuffed Baked Potatoes, 42
Veggie & Chicken Nuggets, 160
Velveeta® Beef Enchiladas Olé, 88
Velveeta® Cheesy Chicken & Rice
  Skillet, 66
Velveeta® 15 Minute Cheesy Rice
  with Ham & Broccoli, 112
Velveeta® Salsa Mac, 98
Velveeta® Salsa Mac 'n' Cheese, 156
Velveeta® Tuna & Noodles, 141
Velveeta® Ultimate Grilled Cheese,
  166
Velveeta® Ultimate Macaroni &
  Cheese, 44

W
Walnut Meringues, 206
White Chocolate
  Dessert Grape Clusters, 184
  Triple Layer Chocolate Mints, 200
Wish-Bone® Marinade Italiano, 64

Z
Zesty Bruschetta, 13
Zesty Peppered Steaks, 84

METRIC CONVERSION CHART

VOLUME MEASUREMENTS (dry)

1/8 teaspoon = 0.5 mL
1/4 teaspoon = 1 mL
1/2 teaspoon = 2 mL
3/4 teaspoon = 4 mL
1 teaspoon = 5 mL
1 tablespoon = 15 mL
2 tablespoons = 30 mL
1/4 cup = 60 mL
1/3 cup = 75 mL
1/2 cup = 125 mL
2/3 cup = 150 mL
3/4 cup = 175 mL
1 cup = 250 mL
2 cups = 1 pint = 500 mL
3 cups = 750 mL
4 cups = 1 quart = 1 L

VOLUME MEASUREMENTS (fluid)

1 fluid ounce (2 tablespoons) = 30 mL
4 fluid ounces (1/2 cup) = 125 mL
8 fluid ounces (1 cup) = 250 mL
12 fluid ounces (1 1/2 cups) = 375 mL
16 fluid ounces (2 cups) = 500 mL

WEIGHTS (mass)

1/2 ounce = 15 g
1 ounce = 30 g
3 ounces = 90 g
4 ounces = 120 g
8 ounces = 225 g
10 ounces = 285 g
12 ounces = 360 g
16 ounces = 1 pound = 450 g

DIMENSIONS

1/16 inch = 2 mm
1/8 inch = 3 mm
1/4 inch = 6 mm
1/2 inch = 1.5 cm
3/4 inch = 2 cm
1 inch = 2.5 cm

OVEN TEMPERATURES

250°F = 120°C
275°F = 140°C
300°F = 150°C
325°F = 160°C
350°F = 180°C
375°F = 190°C
400°F = 200°C
425°F = 220°C
450°F = 230°C

BAKING PAN SIZES

Utensil	Size in Inches/Quarts	Metric Volume	Size in Centimeters
Baking or Cake Pan (square or rectangular)	8×8×2	2 L	20×20×5
	9×9×2	2.5 L	23×23×5
	12×8×2	3 L	30×20×5
	13×9×2	3.5 L	33×23×5
Loaf Pan	8×4×3	1.5 L	20×10×7
	9×5×3	2 L	23×13×7
Round Layer Cake Pan	8×1½	1.2 L	20×4
	9×1½	1.5 L	23×4
Pie Plate	8×1¼	750 mL	20×3
	9×1¼	1 L	23×3
Baking Dish or Casserole	1 quart	1 L	—
	1½ quart	1.5 L	—
	2 quart	2 L	—